MARVEL
ULTIMATE
SPIDER-MAN

MARVEL UNIVERSE ULTIMATE SPIDER-MAN VOL. 6. Contains material originally published in magazine form as MARVEL UNIVERSE ULTIMATE SPIDER-MAN #21-24. First printing 2014. ISBN# 978-0-7851-8815-5. Published by MARVEL WORLDWIDE, INC., a subsidiary of MARVEL ENTERTAINMENT, LLC. OFFICE OF PUBLICATION: 135 West 50th Street, New York, NY 10020. Copyright © 2013 and 2014 Marvel Characters, Inc. All rights reserved. All characters featured in this issue and the distinctive names and likenesses thereof, and all related indicia are trademarks of Marvel Characters, Inc. No similarity between any of the names, characters, persons, and/or institutions in this magazine with those of any living or dead person or institution is intended, and any such similarity which may exist is purely coincidental. **Printed in the U.S.A.** ALAN FINE, EVP - Office of the President, Marvel Worldwide, Inc. and EVP & CMO Marvel Characters B.V.; DAN BUCKLEY, Publisher & President - Print, Animation & Digital Divisions; JOE QUESADA, Chief Creative Officer; TOM BREVOORT, SVP of Publishing; DAVID BOGART, SVP of Operations & Procurement, Publishing; C.B. CEBULSKI, SVP of Creator & Content Development; DAVID GABRIEL, SVP Print, Sales & Marketing; JIM O'KEEFE, VP of Operations & Logistics; DAN CARR, Executive Director of Publishing Technology; SUSAN CRESPI, Editorial Operations Manager; ALEX MORALES, Publishing Operations Manager; STAN LEE, Chairman Emeritus. For information regarding advertising in Marvel Comics or on Marvel.com, please contact Niza Disla, Director of Marvel Partnerships, at ndisla@marvel.com. For Marvel subscription inquiries, please call 800-217-9158. **Manufactured between 4/4/2014 and 5/12/2014 by SHERIDAN BOOKS, INC., CHELSEA, MI, USA.**

10 9 8 7 6 5 4 3 2 1

MARVEL
ULTIMATE SPIDER-MAN

BASED ON THE TV SERIES BY
MAN OF ACTION, JAMES FELDER, BRIAN MICHAEL BENDIS, SCOTT MOSIER & EUGENE SON

ADAPTED BY
JOE CARAMAGNA

EDITOR
SEBASTIAN GIRNER

CONSULTING EDITOR
JON MOISAN

SENIOR EDITOR
MARK PANICCIA

Collection Editor: **Alex Starbuck**
Editors, Special Projects: **Jennifer Grünwald & Mark D. Beazley**
Senior Editor, Special Projects: **Jeff Youngquist**
SVP Print, Sales & Marketing: **David Gabriel**
Head of Marvel Television: **Jeph Loeb**

Editor In Chief: **Axel Alonso**
Chief Creative Officer: **Joe Quesada**
Publisher: **Dan Buckley**
Executive Producer: **Alan Fine**

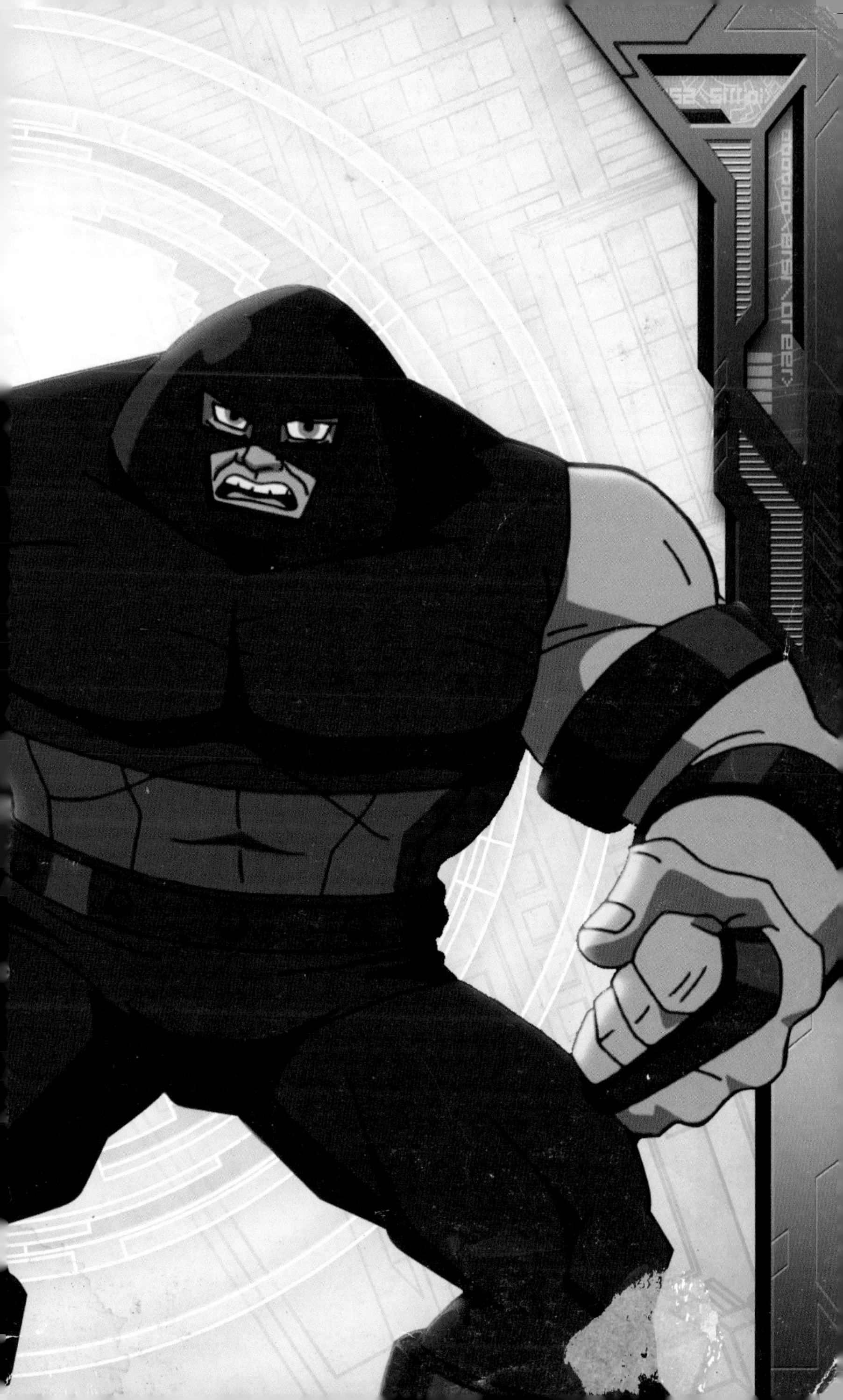

WHILE ATTENDING A DEMONSTRATION IN RADIOLOGY, HIGH SCHOOL STUDENT PETER PARKER WAS BITTEN BY A SPIDER THAT HAD ACCIDENTALLY BEEN EXPOSED TO RADIOACTIVE RAYS. THROUGH A MIRACLE OF SCIENCE, PETER SOON FOUND THAT HE HAD GAINED THE SPIDER'S POWERS...AND HAD, IN EFFECT, BECOME A HUMAN SPIDER! FROM THAT DAY ON, HE HAS ENDEAVORED TO BECOME THE...

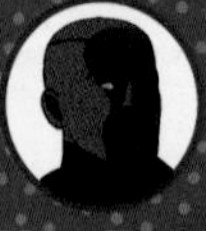
NICK FURY

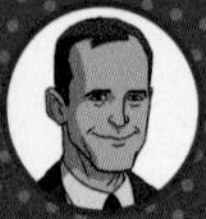
PRINCIPAL COULSON

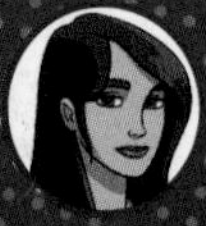
MARY JANE WATSON

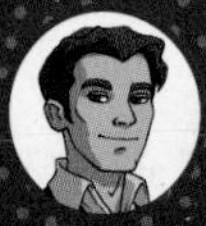
HARRY OSBORN

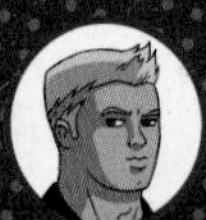
FLASH THOMPSON

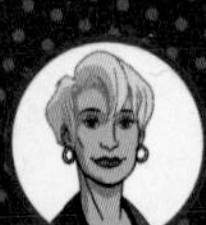
AUNT MAY

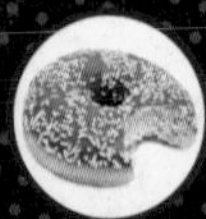
A DONUT (YUM!)

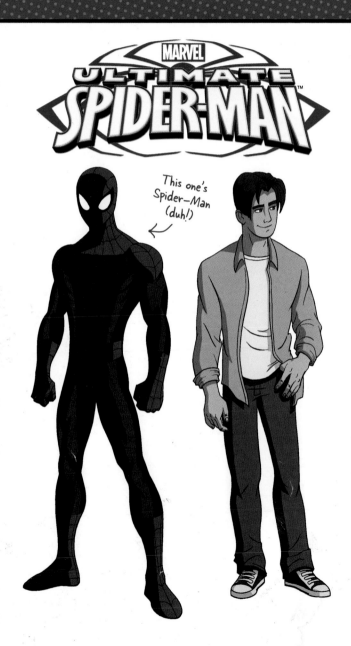

MARVEL ULTIMATE SPIDER-MAN™

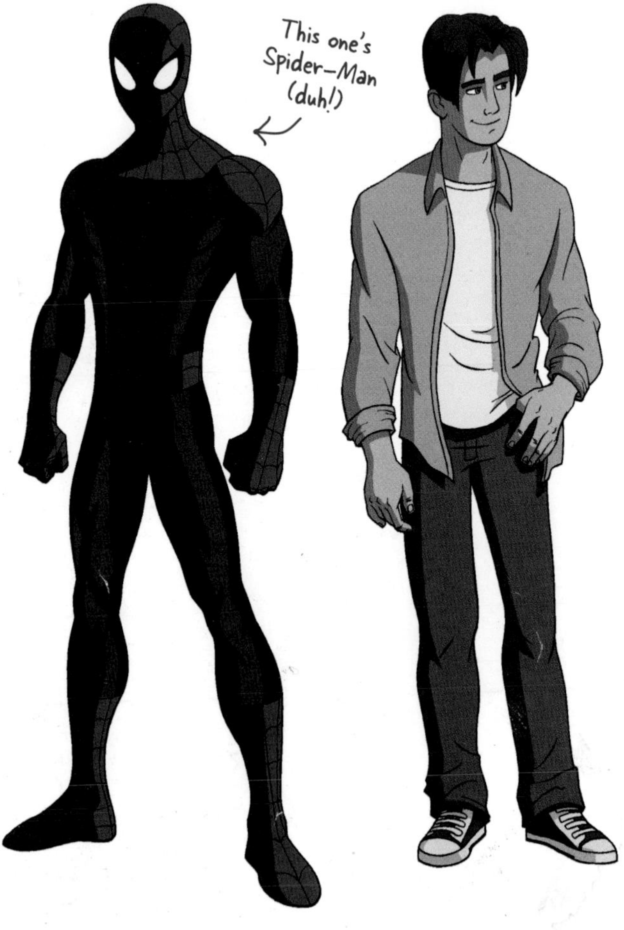
This one's Spider-Man (duh!)

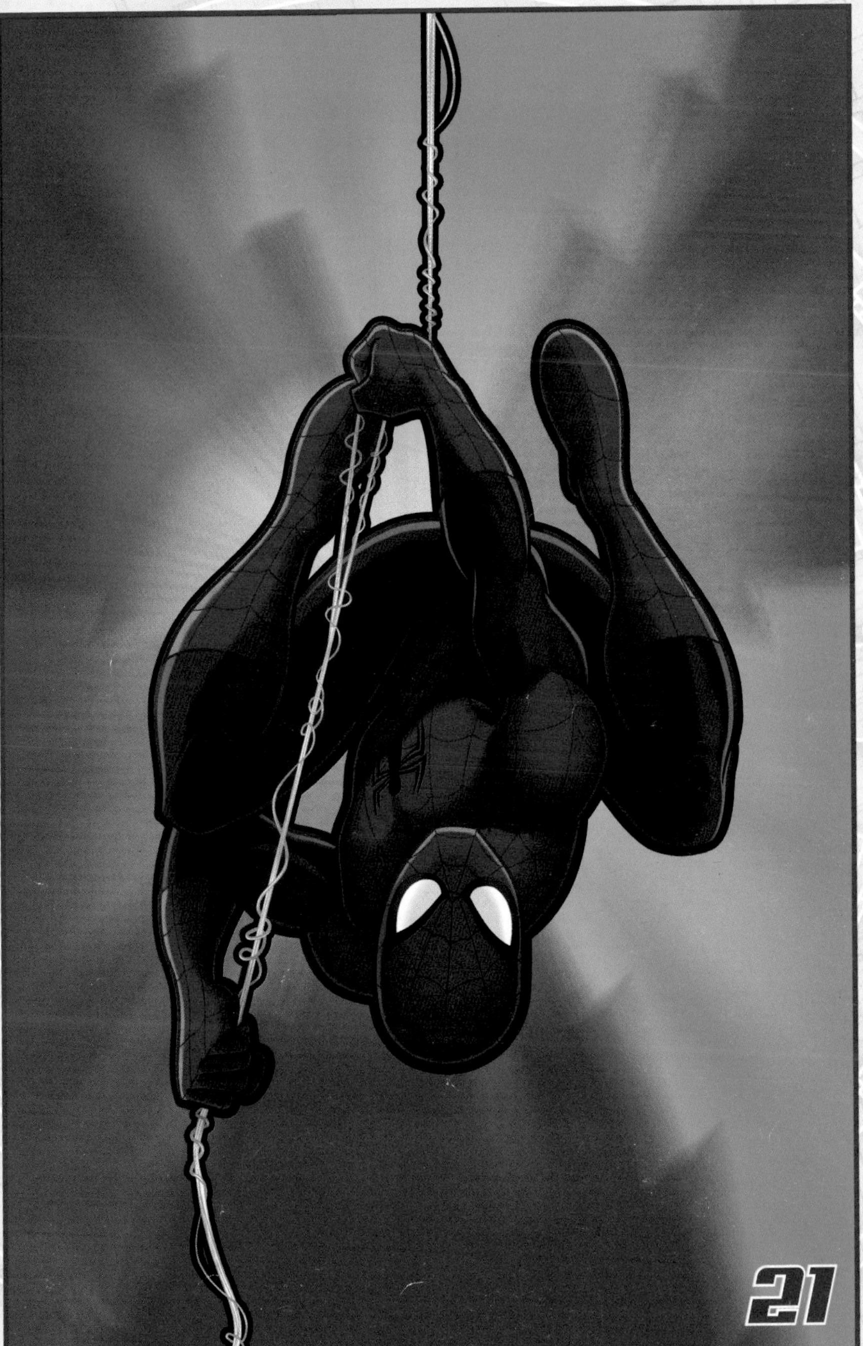
21

Based on "Strange"

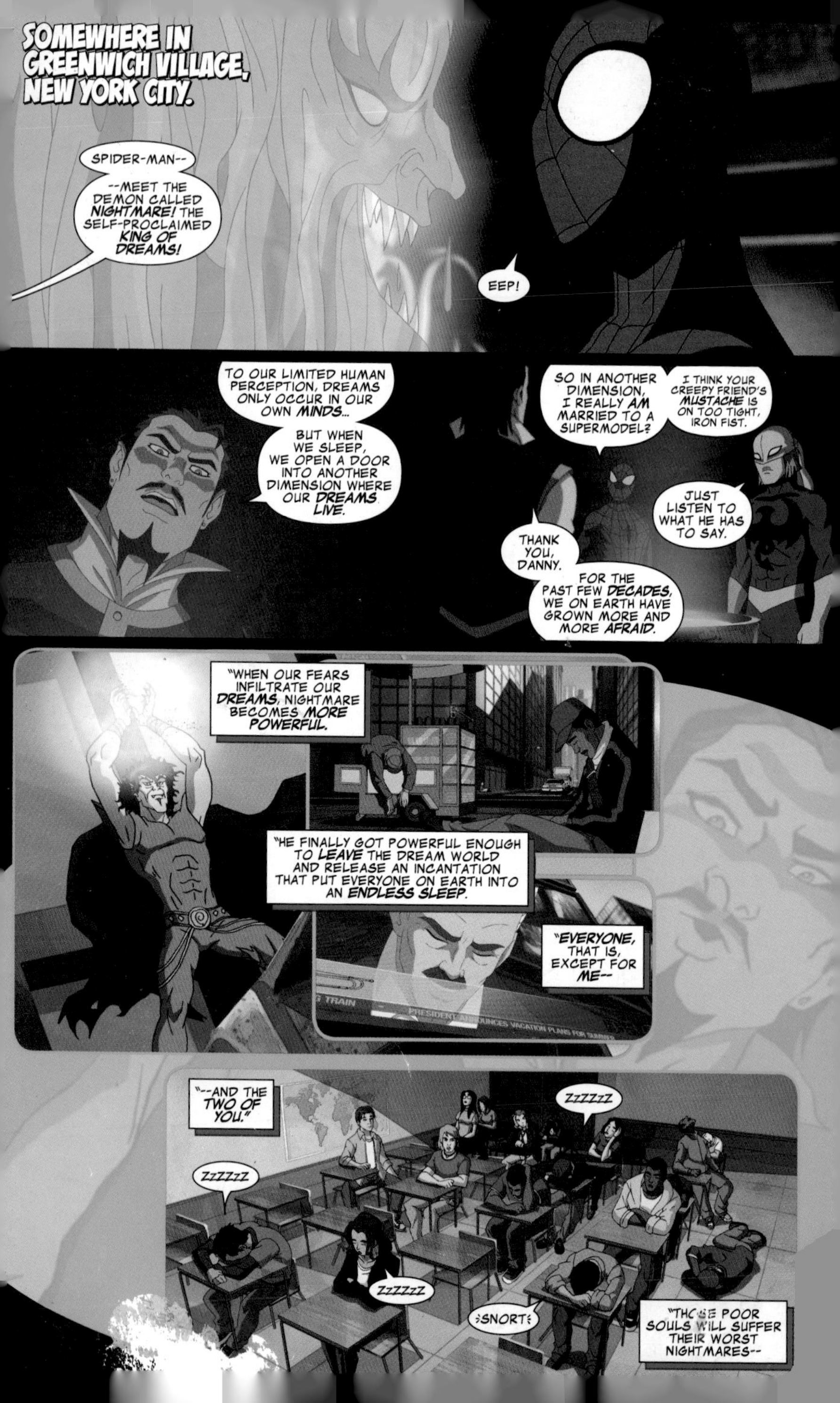

SOMEWHERE IN GREENWICH VILLAGE, NEW YORK CITY.
SPIDER-MAN--
--MEET THE DEMON CALLED NIGHTMARE! THE SELF-PROCLAIMED KING OF DREAMS!
EEP!
TO OUR LIMITED HUMAN PERCEPTION, DREAMS ONLY OCCUR IN OUR OWN MINDS...
BUT WHEN WE SLEEP, WE OPEN A DOOR INTO ANOTHER DIMENSION WHERE OUR DREAMS LIVE.
SO IN ANOTHER DIMENSION, I REALLY AM MARRIED TO A SUPERMODEL?
I THINK YOUR CREEPY FRIEND'S MUSTACHE IS ON TOO TIGHT, IRON FIST.
JUST LISTEN TO WHAT HE HAS TO SAY.
THANK YOU, DANNY.
FOR THE PAST FEW DECADES, WE ON EARTH HAVE GROWN MORE AND MORE AFRAID.
"WHEN OUR FEARS INFILTRATE OUR DREAMS, NIGHTMARE BECOMES MORE POWERFUL.
"HE FINALLY GOT POWERFUL ENOUGH TO LEAVE THE DREAM WORLD AND RELEASE AN INCANTATION THAT PUT EVERYONE ON EARTH INTO AN ENDLESS SLEEP.
"EVERYONE, THAT IS, EXCEPT FOR ME--
"--AND THE TWO OF YOU."
ZZZZZZ
ZZZZZZ
ZZZZZZ
SNORT
"THOSE POOR SOULS WILL SUFFER THEIR WORST NIGHTMARES--

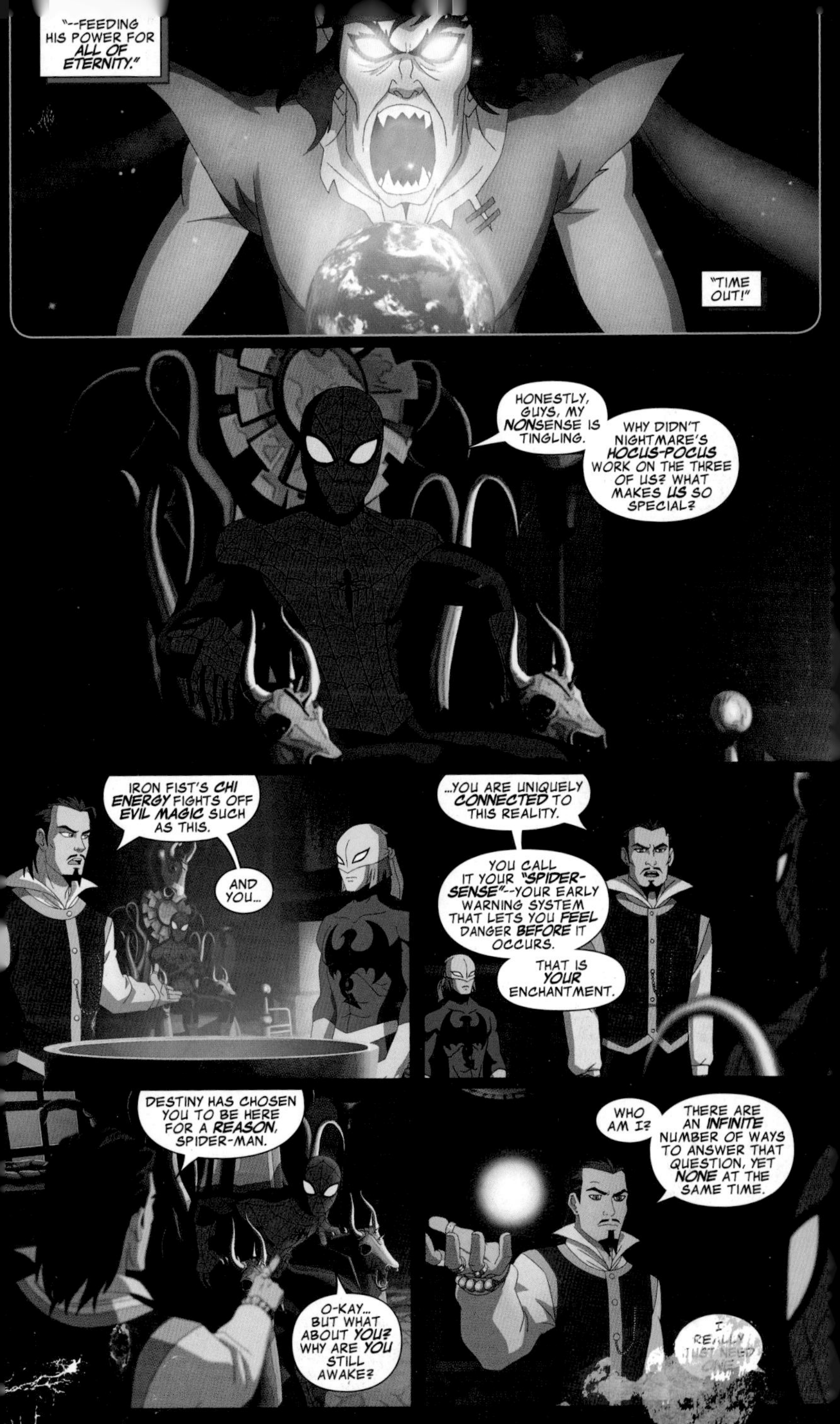

"--FEEDING HIS POWER FOR ALL OF ETERNITY."
"TIME OUT!"
HONESTLY, GUYS, MY NONSENSE IS TINGLING.
WHY DIDN'T NIGHTMARE'S HOCUS-POCUS WORK ON THE THREE OF US? WHAT MAKES US SO SPECIAL?
IRON FIST'S CHI ENERGY FIGHTS OFF EVIL MAGIC SUCH AS THIS.
AND YOU...
...YOU ARE UNIQUELY CONNECTED TO THIS REALITY.
YOU CALL IT YOUR "SPIDER-SENSE"--YOUR EARLY WARNING SYSTEM THAT LETS YOU FEEL DANGER BEFORE IT OCCURS.
THAT IS YOUR ENCHANTMENT.
DESTINY HAS CHOSEN YOU TO BE HERE FOR A REASON, SPIDER-MAN.
O-KAY... BUT WHAT ABOUT YOU? WHY ARE YOU STILL AWAKE?
WHO AM I?
THERE ARE AN INFINITE NUMBER OF WAYS TO ANSWER THAT QUESTION, YET NONE AT THE SAME TIME.
I REALLY JUST NEED ONE.

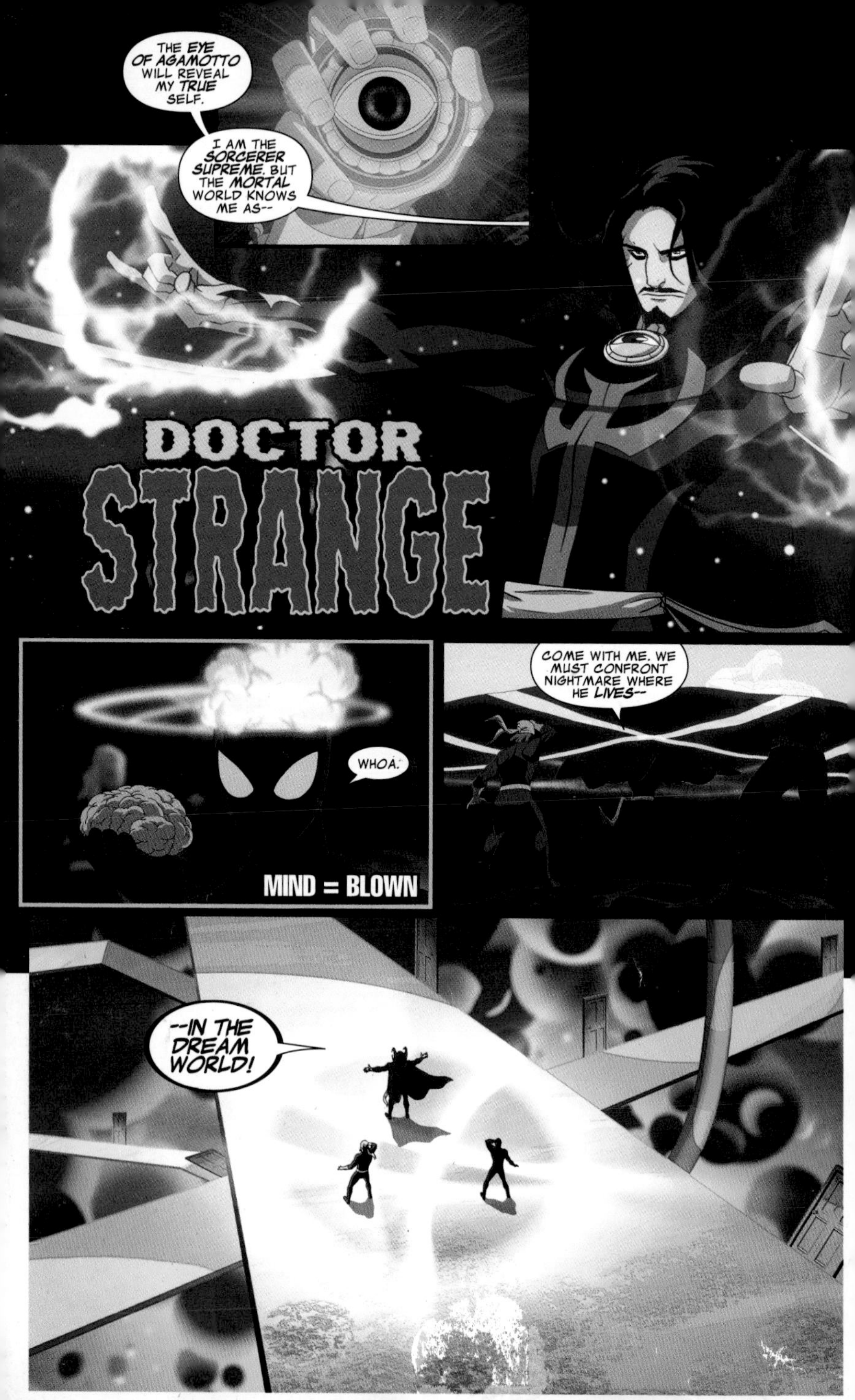
THE EYE OF AGAMOTTO WILL REVEAL MY TRUE SELF.
I AM THE SORCERER SUPREME. BUT THE MORTAL WORLD KNOWS ME AS--
DOCTOR STRANGE
WHOA.
MIND = BLOWN
COME WITH ME. WE MUST CONFRONT NIGHTMARE WHERE HE LIVES--
--IN THE DREAM WORLD!

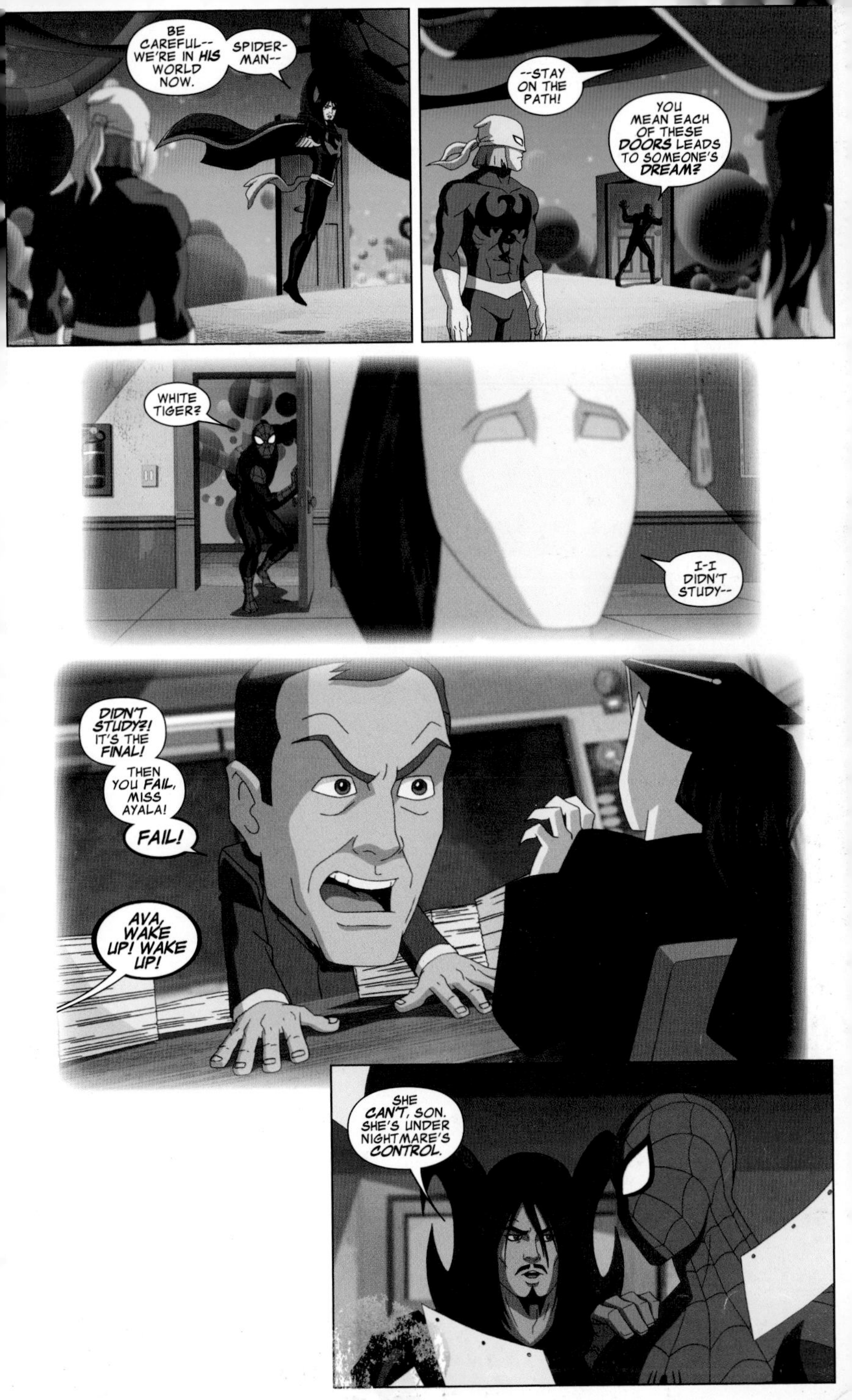
BE CAREFUL-- WE'RE IN HIS WORLD NOW.
SPIDER-MAN--
--STAY ON THE PATH!
YOU MEAN EACH OF THESE DOORS LEADS TO SOMEONE'S DREAM?
WHITE TIGER?
I-I DIDN'T STUDY--
DIDN'T STUDY?! IT'S THE FINAL!
THEN YOU FAIL, MISS AYALA!
FAIL!
AVA, WAKE UP! WAKE UP!
SHE CAN'T, SON. SHE'S UNDER NIGHTMARE'S CONTROL.

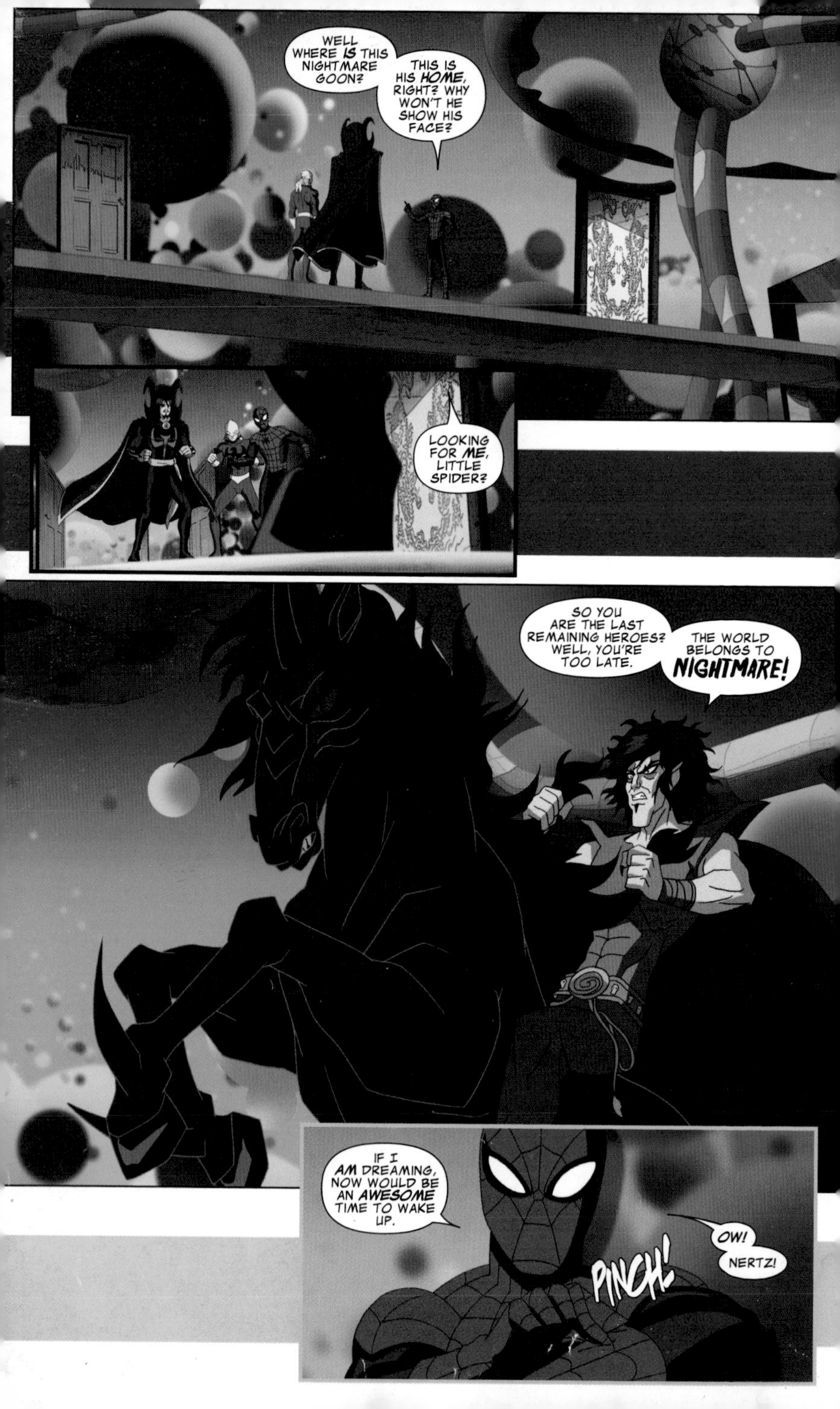
WELL WHERE IS THIS NIGHTMARE GOON?
THIS IS HIS HOME, RIGHT? WHY WON'T HE SHOW HIS FACE?
LOOKING FOR ME, LITTLE SPIDER?
SO YOU ARE THE LAST REMAINING HEROES? WELL, YOU'RE TOO LATE.
THE WORLD BELONGS TO NIGHTMARE!
IF I AM DREAMING, NOW WOULD BE AN AWESOME TIME TO WAKE UP.
PINCH!
OW!
NERTZ!

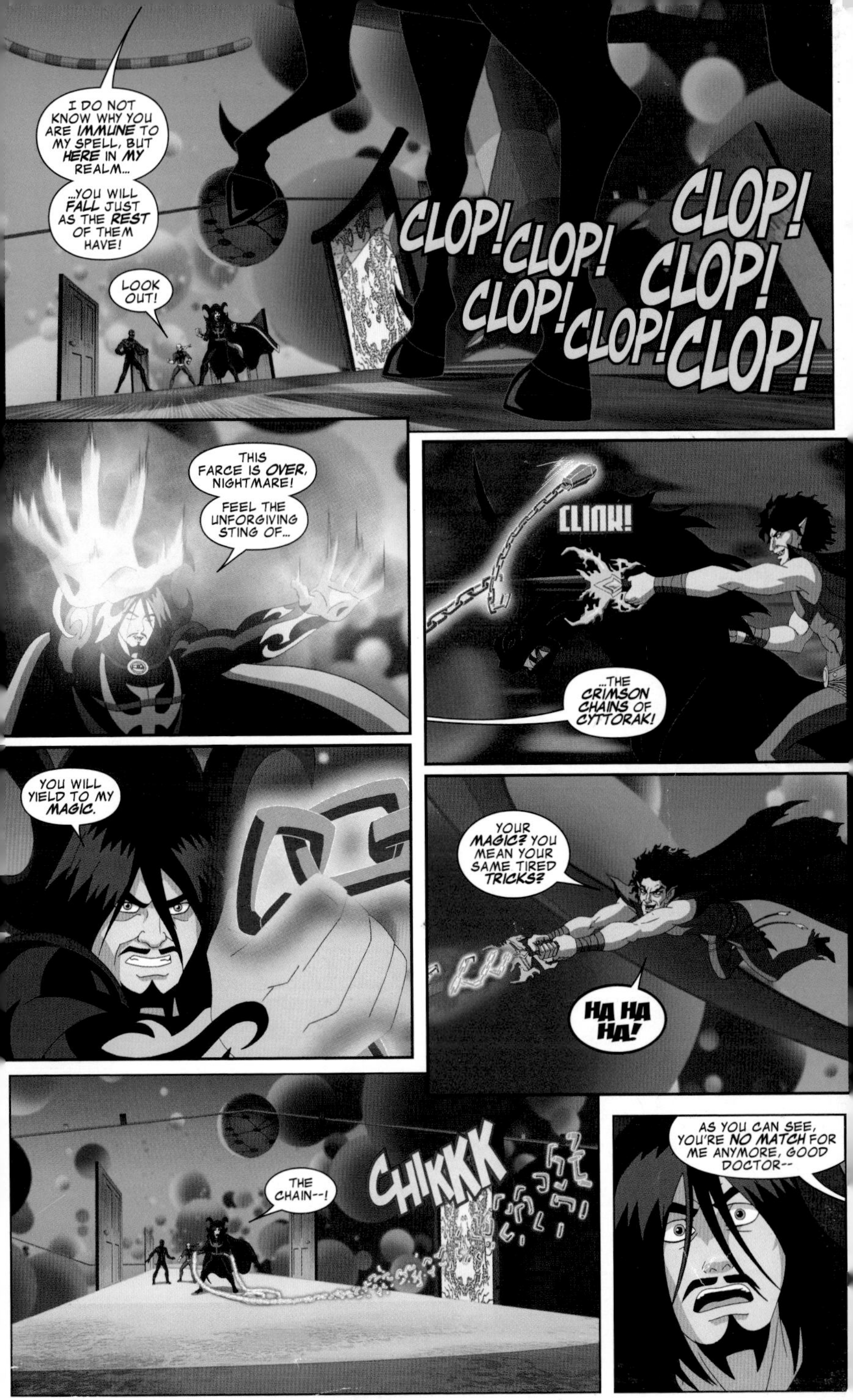
I DO NOT KNOW WHY YOU ARE IMMUNE TO MY SPELL, BUT HERE IN MY REALM...
...YOU WILL FALL JUST AS THE REST OF THEM HAVE!
LOOK OUT!
CLOP! CLOP! CLOP! CLOP! CLOP! CLOP! CLOP!
THIS FARCE IS OVER, NIGHTMARE!
FEEL THE UNFORGIVING STING OF...
CLINK!
...THE CRIMSON CHAINS OF CYTTORAK!
YOU WILL YIELD TO MY MAGIC.
YOUR MAGIC? YOU MEAN YOUR SAME TIRED TRICKS?
HA HA HA!
THE CHAIN--!
CHIKKK
AS YOU CAN SEE, YOU'RE NO MATCH FOR ME ANYMORE, GOOD DOCTOR--

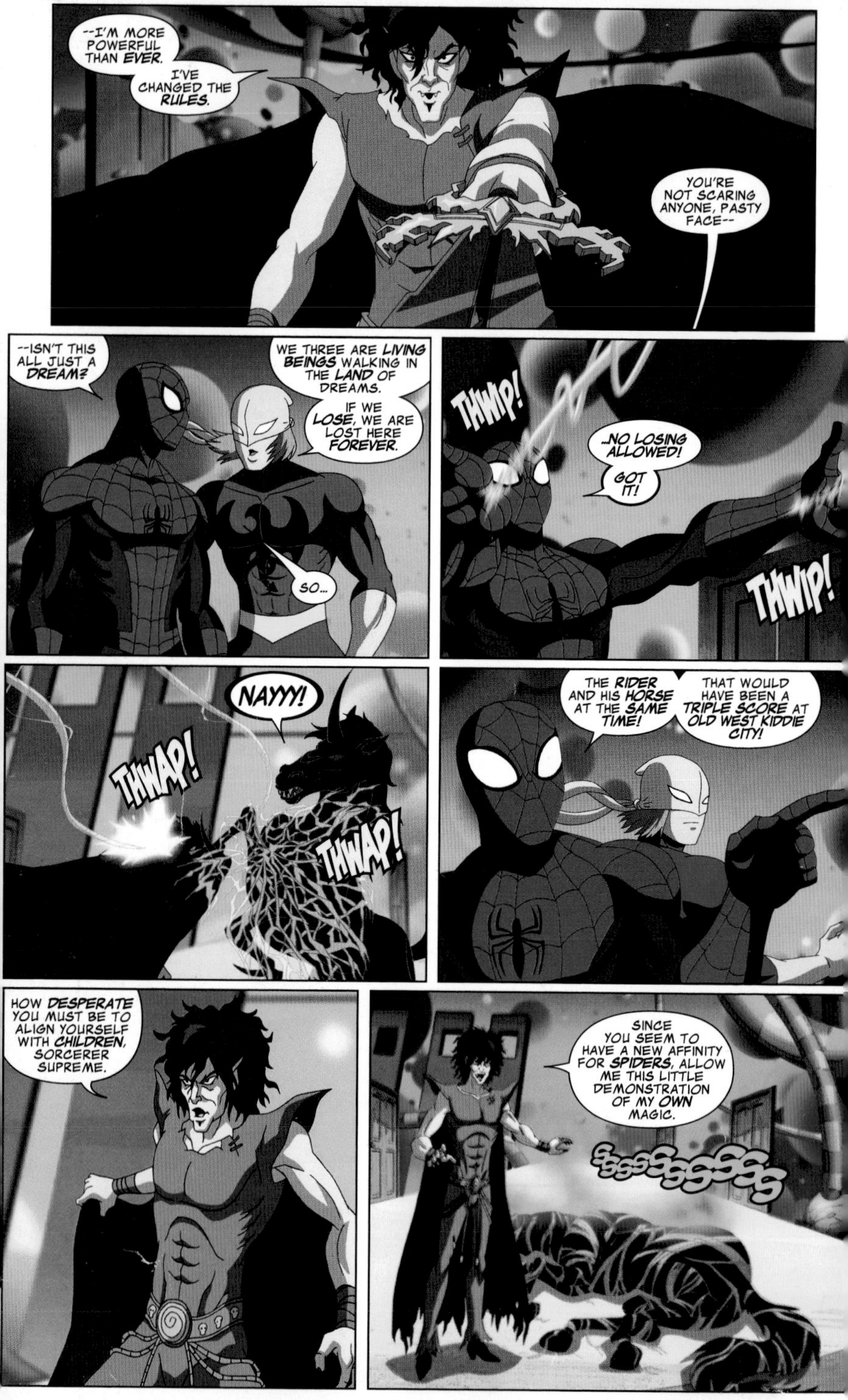
--I'M MORE POWERFUL THAN EVER.
I'VE CHANGED THE RULES.
YOU'RE NOT SCARING ANYONE, PASTY FACE--
--ISN'T THIS ALL JUST A DREAM?
WE THREE ARE LIVING BEINGS WALKING IN THE LAND OF DREAMS.
IF WE LOSE, WE ARE LOST HERE FOREVER.
SO...
THWIP!
...NO LOSING ALLOWED!
GOT IT!
THWIP!
NAYYY!
THWAP!
THWAP!
THE RIDER AND HIS HORSE AT THE SAME TIME!
THAT WOULD HAVE BEEN A TRIPLE SCORE AT OLD WEST KIDDIE CITY!
HOW DESPERATE YOU MUST BE TO ALIGN YOURSELF WITH CHILDREN, SORCERER SUPREME.
SINCE YOU SEEM TO HAVE A NEW AFFINITY FOR SPIDERS, ALLOW ME THIS LITTLE DEMONSTRATION OF MY OWN MAGIC.
SSSSSSSSSSS

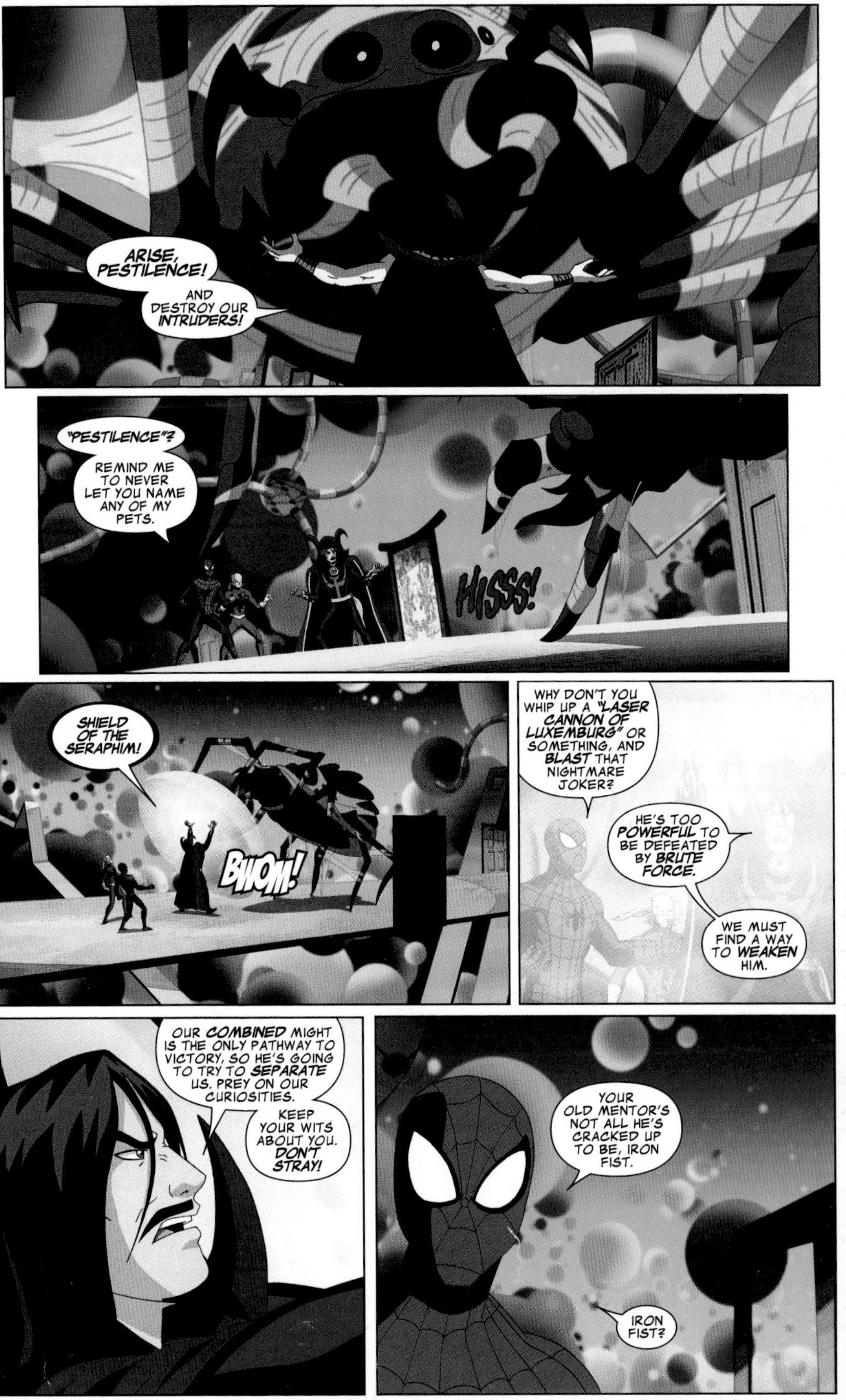
ARISE, PESTILENCE!
AND DESTROY OUR INTRUDERS!
"PESTILENCE"? REMIND ME TO NEVER LET YOU NAME ANY OF MY PETS.
HISSS!
SHIELD OF THE SERAPHIM!
BWOM!
WHY DON'T YOU WHIP UP A "LASER CANNON OF LUXEMBURG" OR SOMETHING, AND BLAST THAT NIGHTMARE JOKER?
HE'S TOO POWERFUL TO BE DEFEATED BY BRUTE FORCE.
WE MUST FIND A WAY TO WEAKEN HIM.
OUR COMBINED MIGHT IS THE ONLY PATHWAY TO VICTORY, SO HE'S GOING TO TRY TO SEPARATE US. PREY ON OUR CURIOSITIES.
KEEP YOUR WITS ABOUT YOU. DON'T STRAY!
YOUR OLD MENTOR'S NOT ALL HE'S CRACKED UP TO BE, IRON FIST.
IRON FIST?

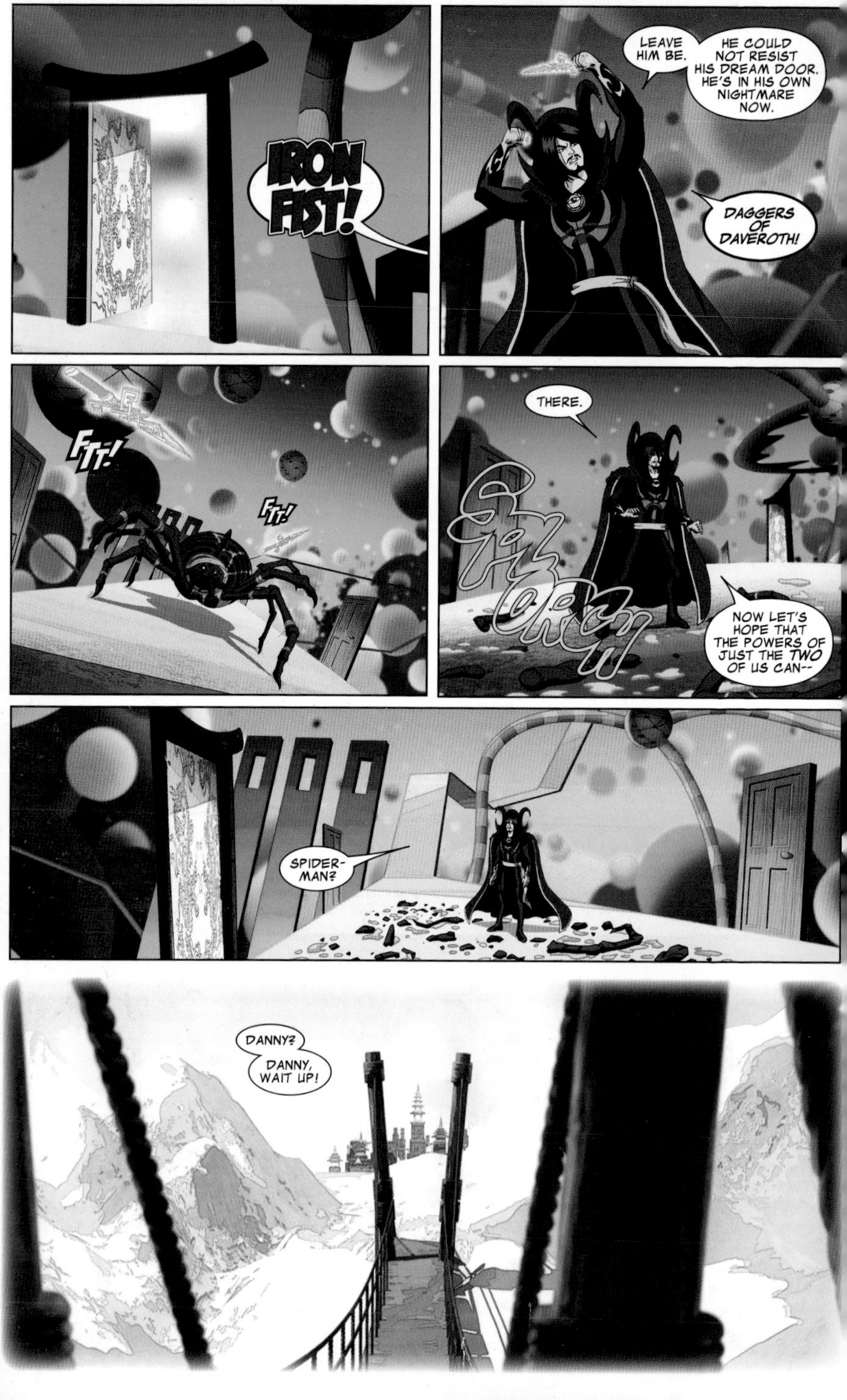
IRON FIST!
LEAVE HIM BE.
HE COULD NOT RESIST HIS DREAM DOOR. HE'S IN HIS OWN NIGHTMARE NOW.
DAGGERS OF DAVEROTH!
FTT!
FTT!
THERE.
NOW LET'S HOPE THAT THE POWERS OF JUST THE TWO OF US CAN--
SPIDER-MAN?
DANNY?
DANNY, WAIT UP!

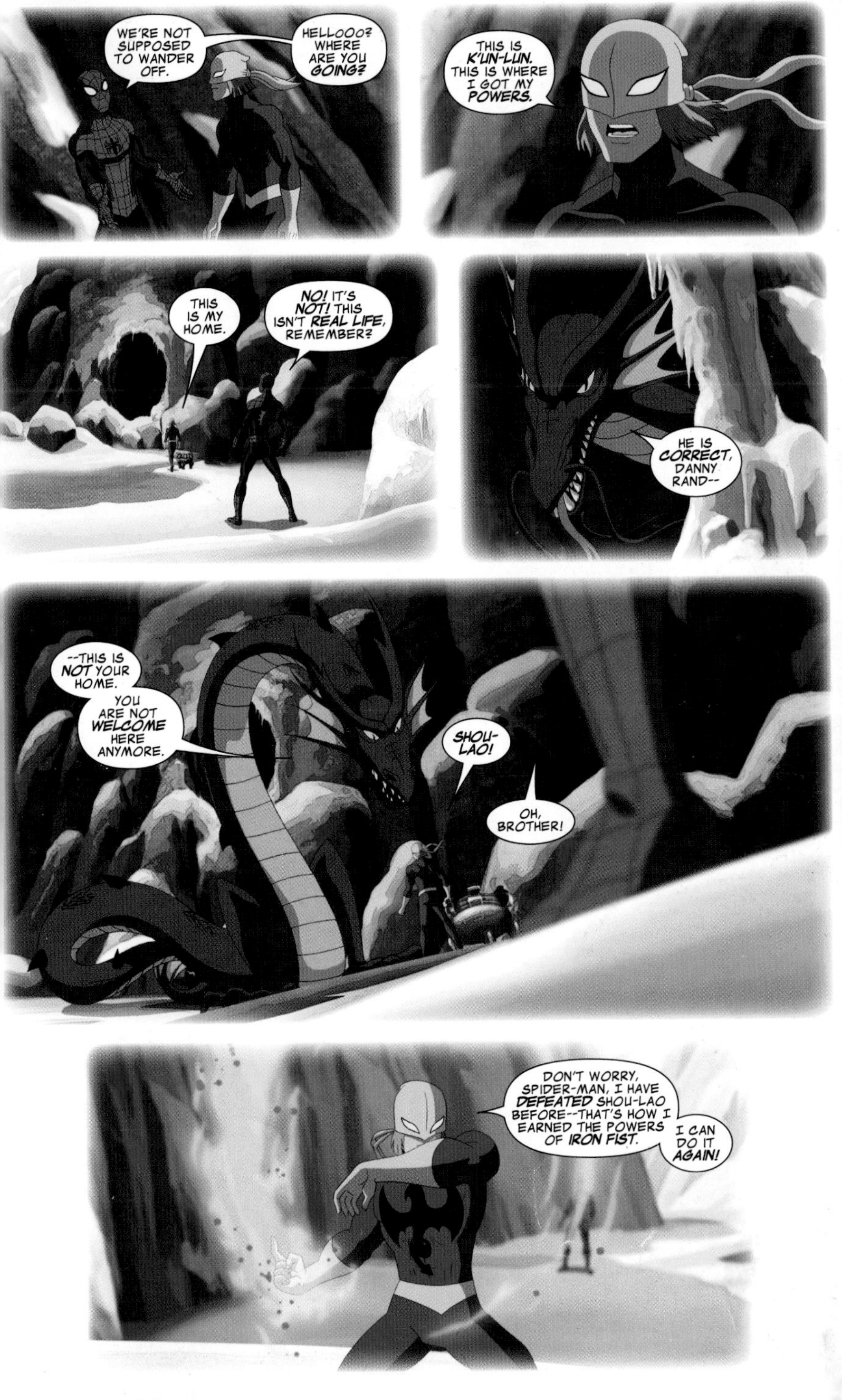

WE'RE NOT SUPPOSED TO WANDER OFF.
HELLOOO? WHERE ARE YOU GOING?
THIS IS K'UN-LUN. THIS IS WHERE I GOT MY POWERS.
THIS IS MY HOME.
NO! IT'S NOT! THIS ISN'T REAL LIFE, REMEMBER?
HE IS CORRECT, DANNY RAND--
--THIS IS NOT YOUR HOME.
YOU ARE NOT WELCOME HERE ANYMORE.
SHOU-LAO!
OH, BROTHER!
DON'T WORRY, SPIDER-MAN, I HAVE DEFEATED SHOU-LAO BEFORE--THAT'S HOW I EARNED THE POWERS OF IRON FIST.
I CAN DO IT AGAIN!

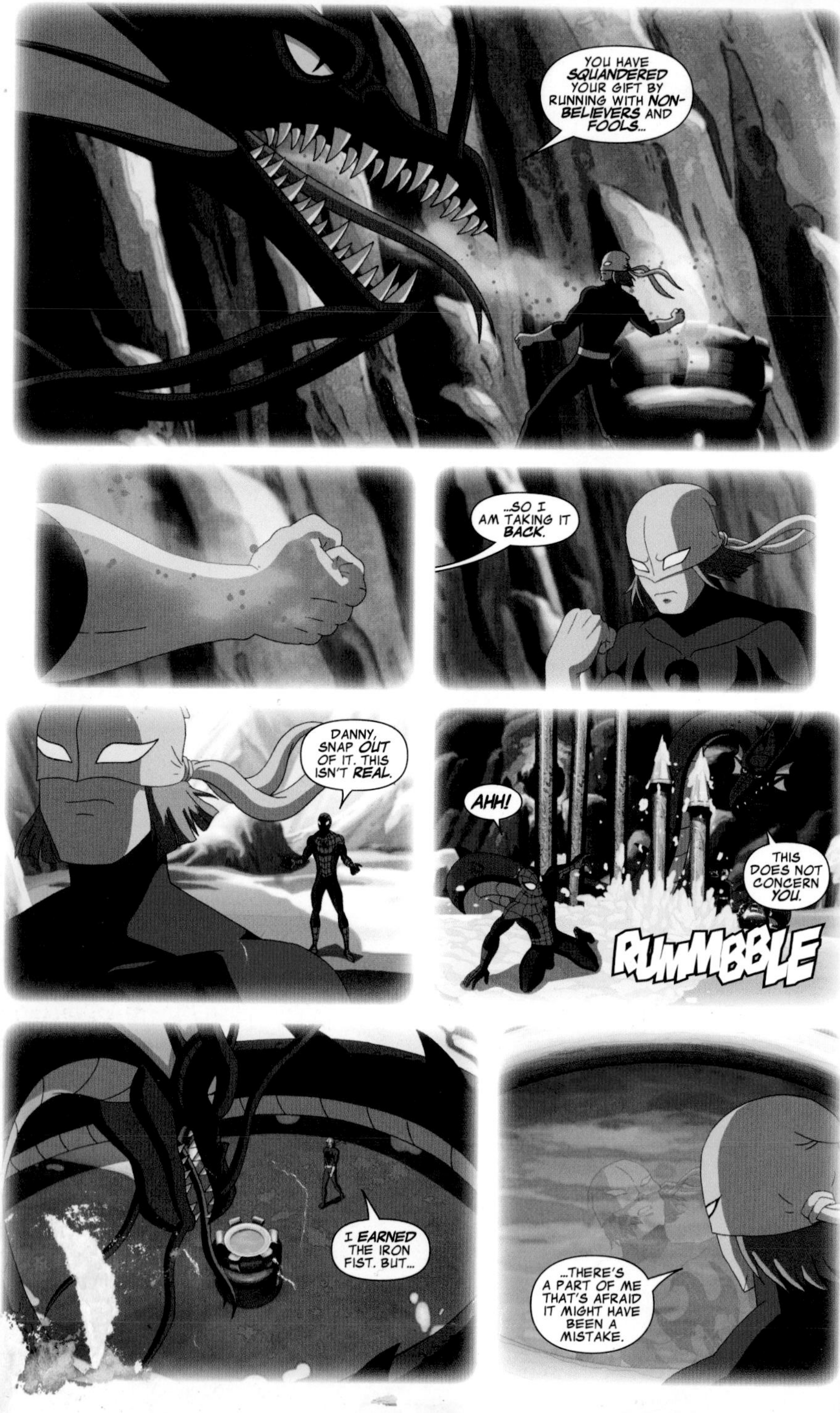

YOU HAVE SQUANDERED YOUR GIFT BY RUNNING WITH NON-BELIEVERS AND FOOLS...
...SO I AM TAKING IT BACK.
DANNY, SNAP OUT OF IT. THIS ISN'T REAL.
AHH!
THIS DOES NOT CONCERN YOU.
RUMMBBLE
I EARNED THE IRON FIST. BUT...
...THERE'S A PART OF ME THAT'S AFRAID IT MIGHT HAVE BEEN A MISTAKE.

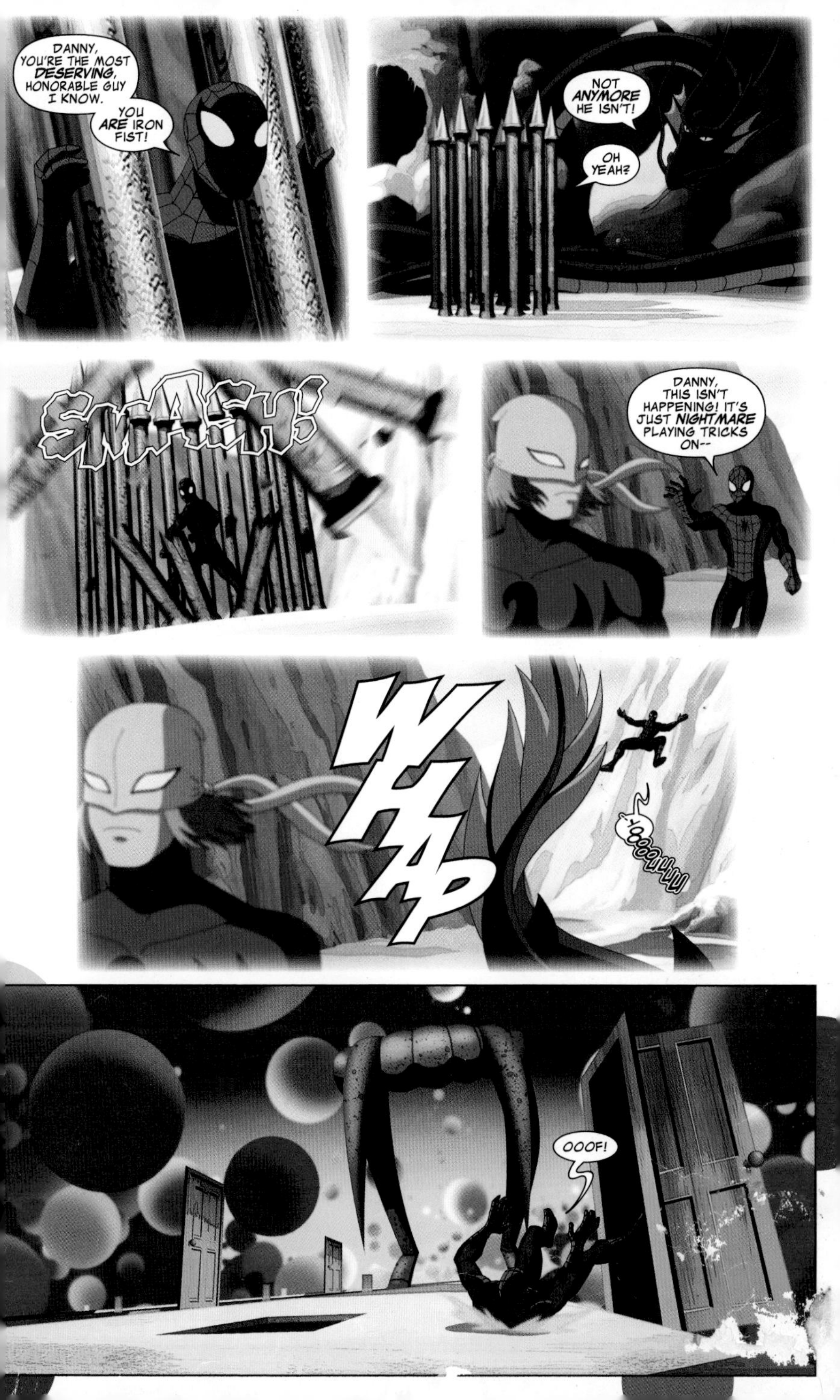
DANNY, YOU'RE THE MOST DESERVING, HONORABLE GUY I KNOW.
YOU ARE IRON FIST!
NOT ANYMORE HE ISN'T!
OH YEAH?
SMASH!
DANNY, THIS ISN'T HAPPENING! IT'S JUST NIGHTMARE PLAYING TRICKS ON--
WHAP
OOOF!

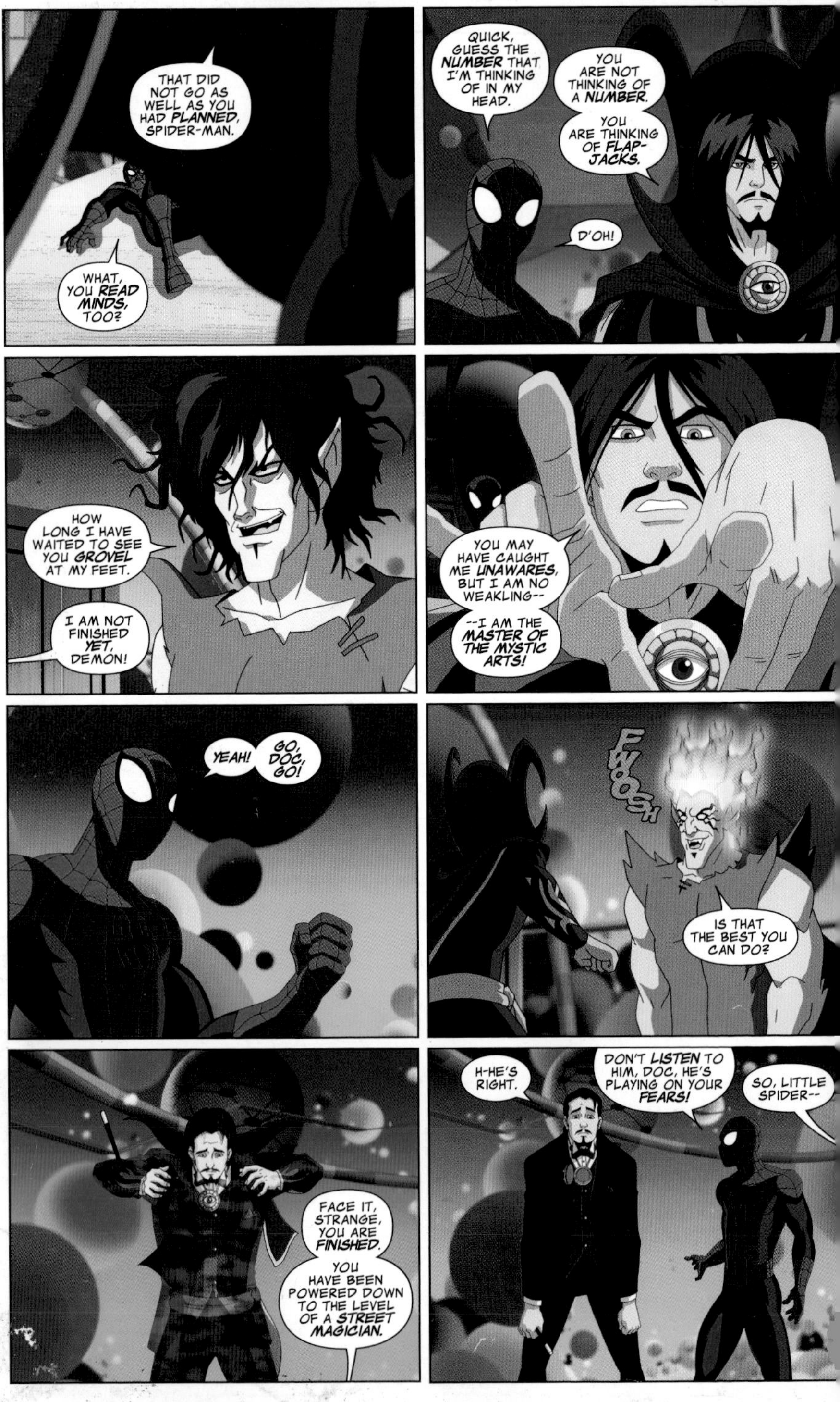

THAT DID NOT GO AS WELL AS YOU HAD PLANNED, SPIDER-MAN.
WHAT, YOU READ MINDS, TOO?
QUICK, GUESS THE NUMBER THAT I'M THINKING OF IN MY HEAD.
YOU ARE NOT THINKING OF A NUMBER.
YOU ARE THINKING OF FLAP-JACKS.
D'OH!
HOW LONG I HAVE WAITED TO SEE YOU GROVEL AT MY FEET.
I AM NOT FINISHED YET, DEMON!
YOU MAY HAVE CAUGHT ME UNAWARES, BUT I AM NO WEAKLING--
--I AM THE MASTER OF THE MYSTIC ARTS!
YEAH!
GO, DOC, GO!
FWOOSH
IS THAT THE BEST YOU CAN DO?
FACE IT, STRANGE, YOU ARE FINISHED.
YOU HAVE BEEN POWERED DOWN TO THE LEVEL OF A STREET MAGICIAN.
H-HE'S RIGHT.
DON'T LISTEN TO HIM, DOC, HE'S PLAYING ON YOUR FEARS!
SO, LITTLE SPIDER--

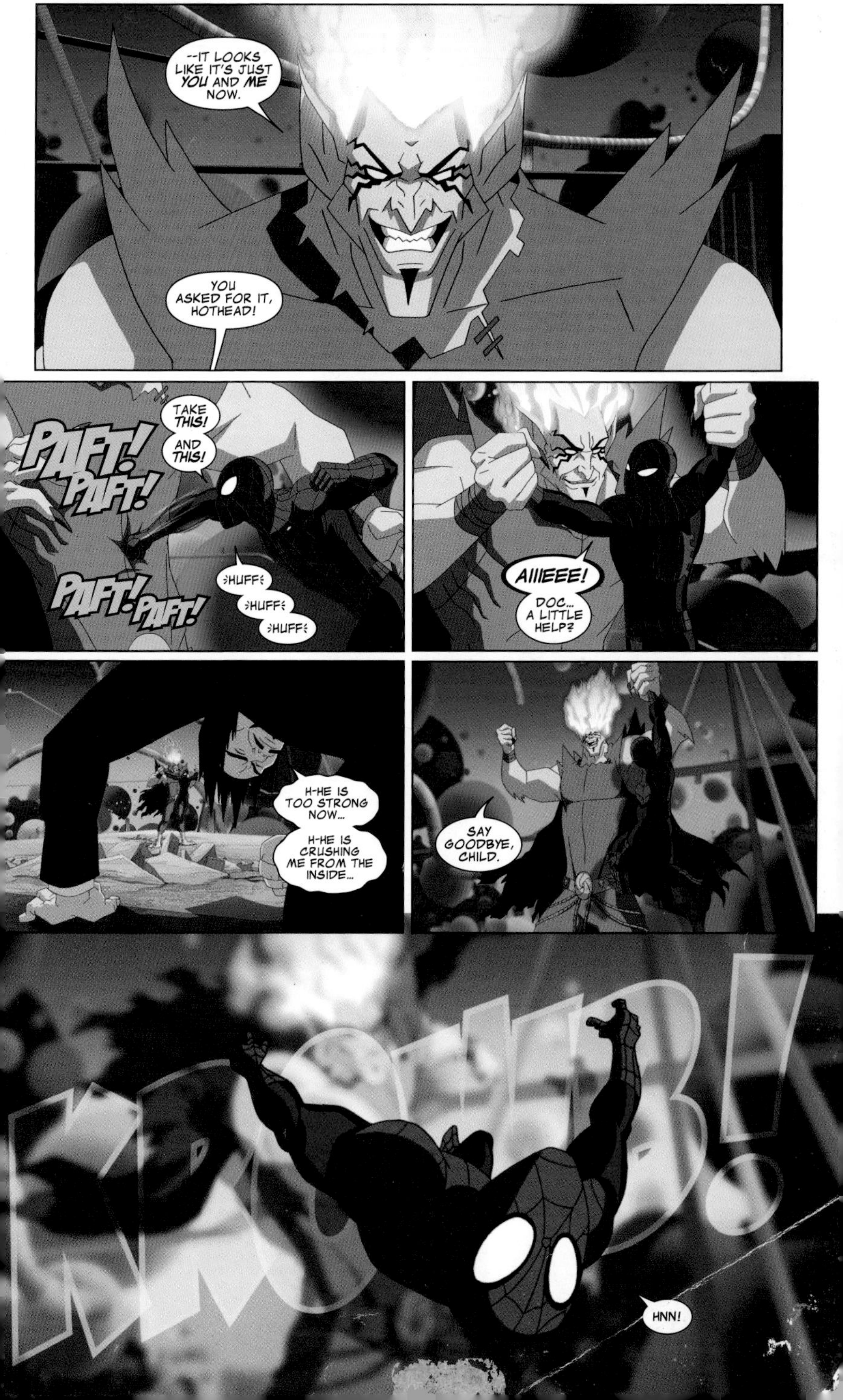
--IT LOOKS LIKE IT'S JUST YOU AND ME NOW.
YOU ASKED FOR IT, HOTHEAD!
TAKE THIS!
AND THIS!
PAFT! PAFT!
PAFT! PAFT!
HUFF
HUFF
HUFF
AIIIEEE!
DOC... A LITTLE HELP?
H-HE IS TOO STRONG NOW...
H-HE IS CRUSHING ME FROM THE INSIDE...
SAY GOODBYE, CHILD.
HNN!

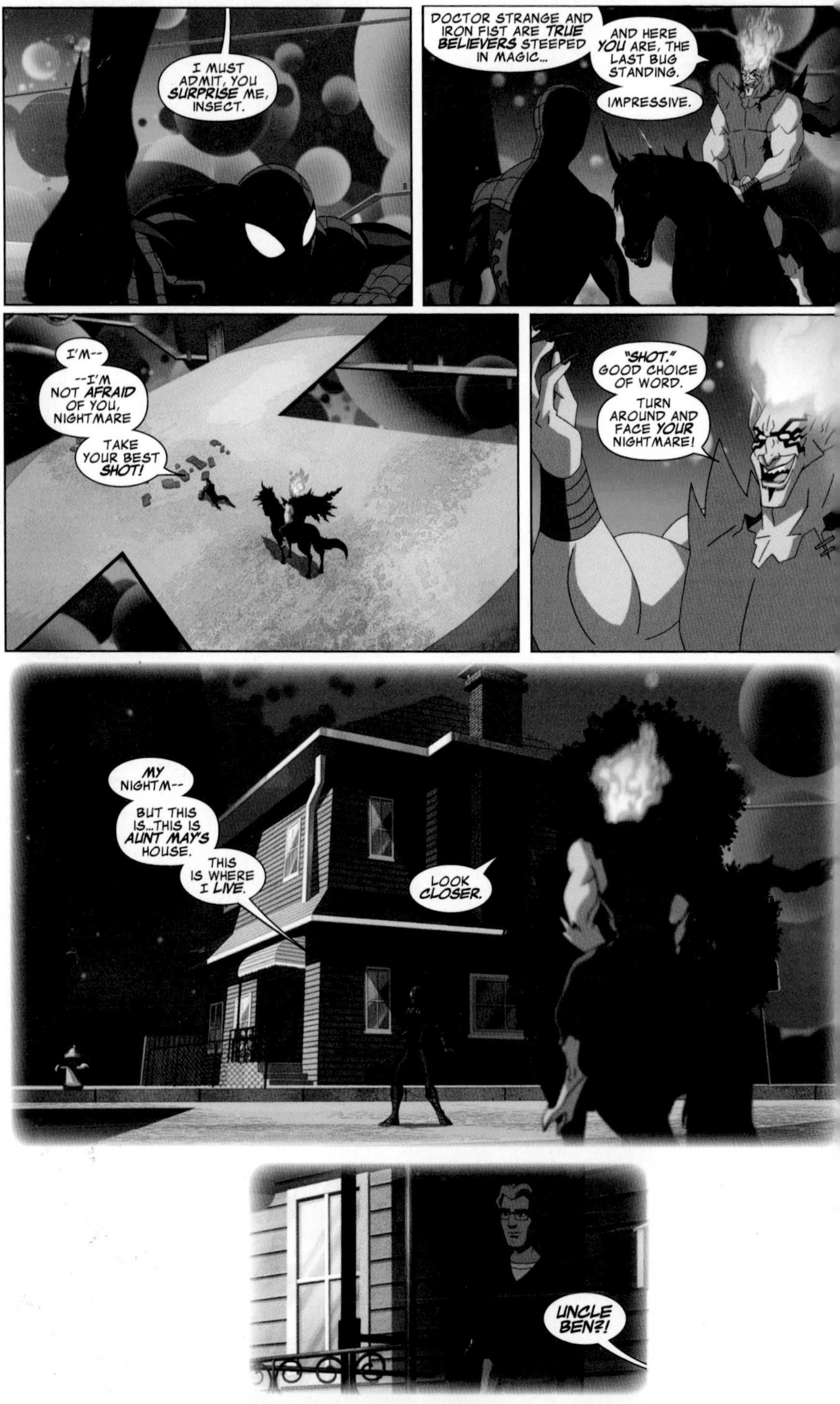
I MUST ADMIT, YOU SURPRISE ME, INSECT.
DOCTOR STRANGE AND IRON FIST ARE TRUE BELIEVERS STEEPED IN MAGIC...
AND HERE YOU ARE, THE LAST BUG STANDING.
IMPRESSIVE.
I'M--
--I'M NOT AFRAID OF YOU, NIGHTMARE
TAKE YOUR BEST SHOT!
"SHOT." GOOD CHOICE OF WORD.
TURN AROUND AND FACE YOUR NIGHTMARE!
MY NIGHTM--
BUT THIS IS...THIS IS AUNT MAY'S HOUSE.
THIS IS WHERE I LIVE.
LOOK CLOSER.
UNCLE BEN?!

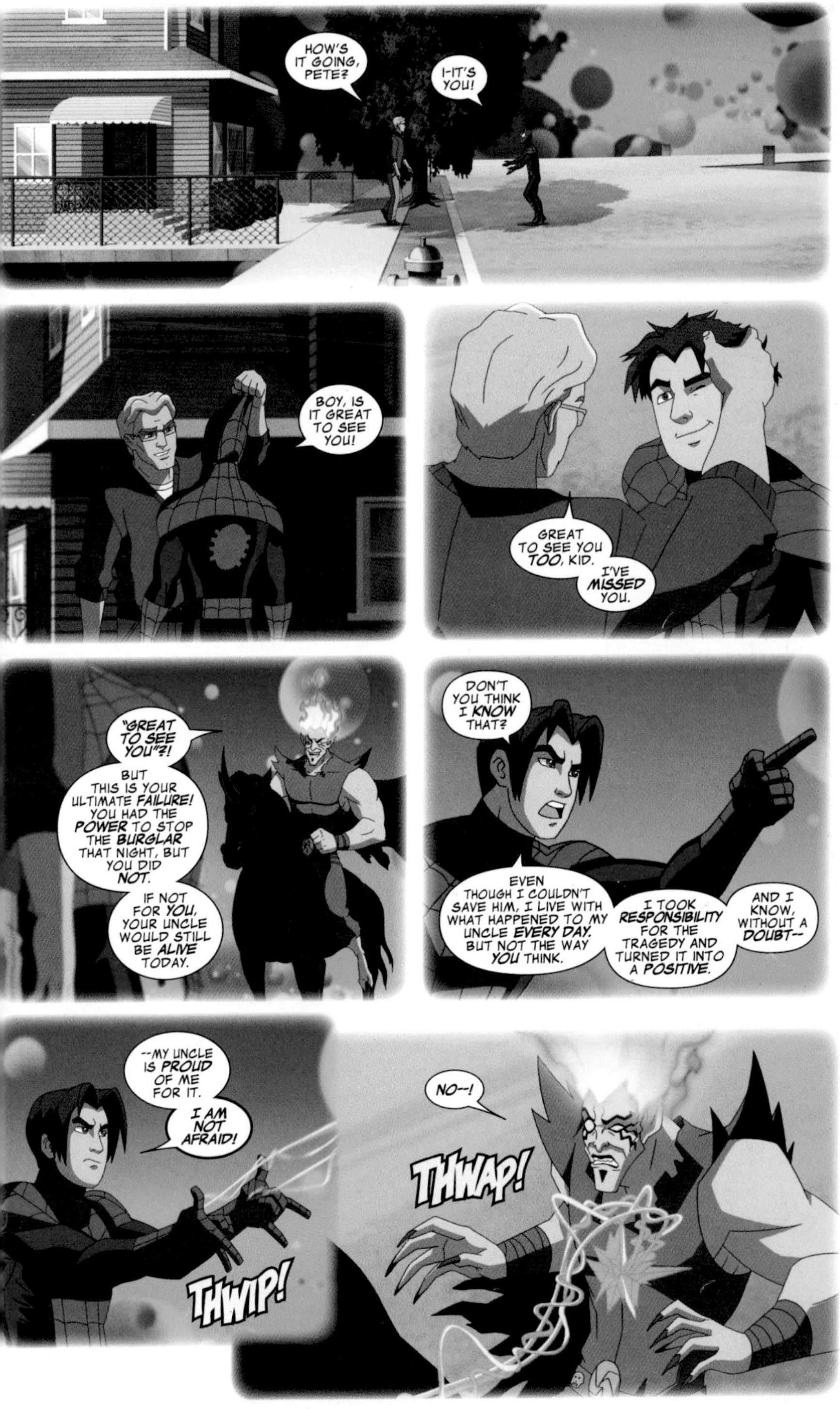
HOW'S IT GOING, PETE?
I-IT'S YOU!
BOY, IS IT GREAT TO SEE YOU!
GREAT TO SEE YOU TOO, KID.
I'VE MISSED YOU.
"GREAT TO SEE YOU"?!
BUT THIS IS YOUR ULTIMATE FAILURE! YOU HAD THE POWER TO STOP THE BURGLAR THAT NIGHT, BUT YOU DID NOT.
IF NOT FOR YOU, YOUR UNCLE WOULD STILL BE ALIVE TODAY.
DON'T YOU THINK I KNOW THAT?
EVEN THOUGH I COULDN'T SAVE HIM, I LIVE WITH WHAT HAPPENED TO MY UNCLE EVERY DAY. BUT NOT THE WAY YOU THINK.
I TOOK RESPONSIBILITY FOR THE TRAGEDY AND TURNED IT INTO A POSITIVE.
AND I KNOW, WITHOUT A DOUBT--
--MY UNCLE IS PROUD OF ME FOR IT.
I AM NOT AFRAID!
THWIP!
NO--!
THWAP!

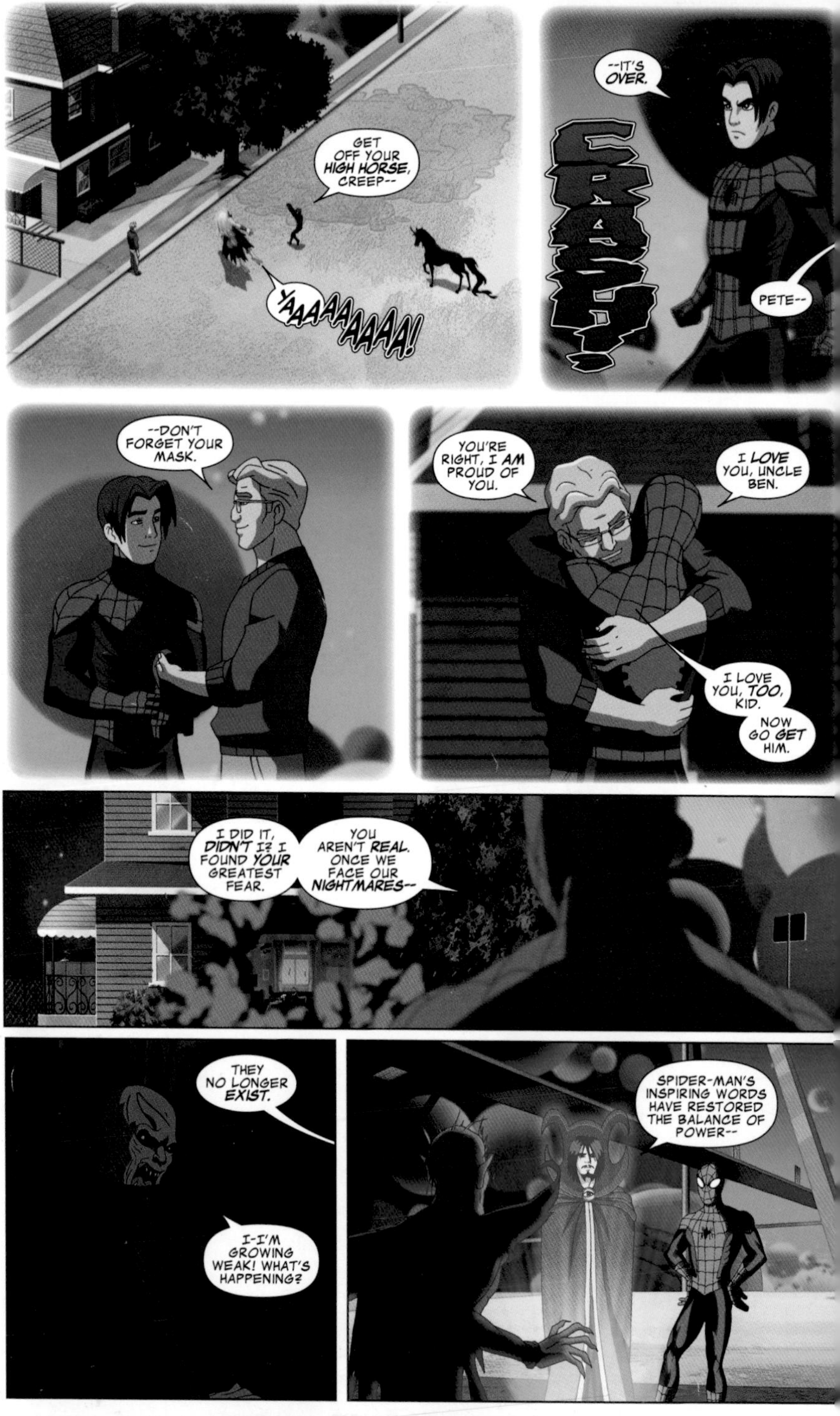
GET OFF YOUR HIGH HORSE, CREEP--
YAAAAAAAAA!
--IT'S OVER.
CRASH!
PETE--
--DON'T FORGET YOUR MASK.
YOU'RE RIGHT, I AM PROUD OF YOU.
I LOVE YOU, UNCLE BEN.
I LOVE YOU, TOO, KID.
NOW GO GET HIM.
I DID IT, DIDN'T I? I FOUND YOUR GREATEST FEAR.
YOU AREN'T REAL. ONCE WE FACE OUR NIGHTMARES--
THEY NO LONGER EXIST.
I-I'M GROWING WEAK! WHAT'S HAPPENING?
SPIDER-MAN'S INSPIRING WORDS HAVE RESTORED THE BALANCE OF POWER--

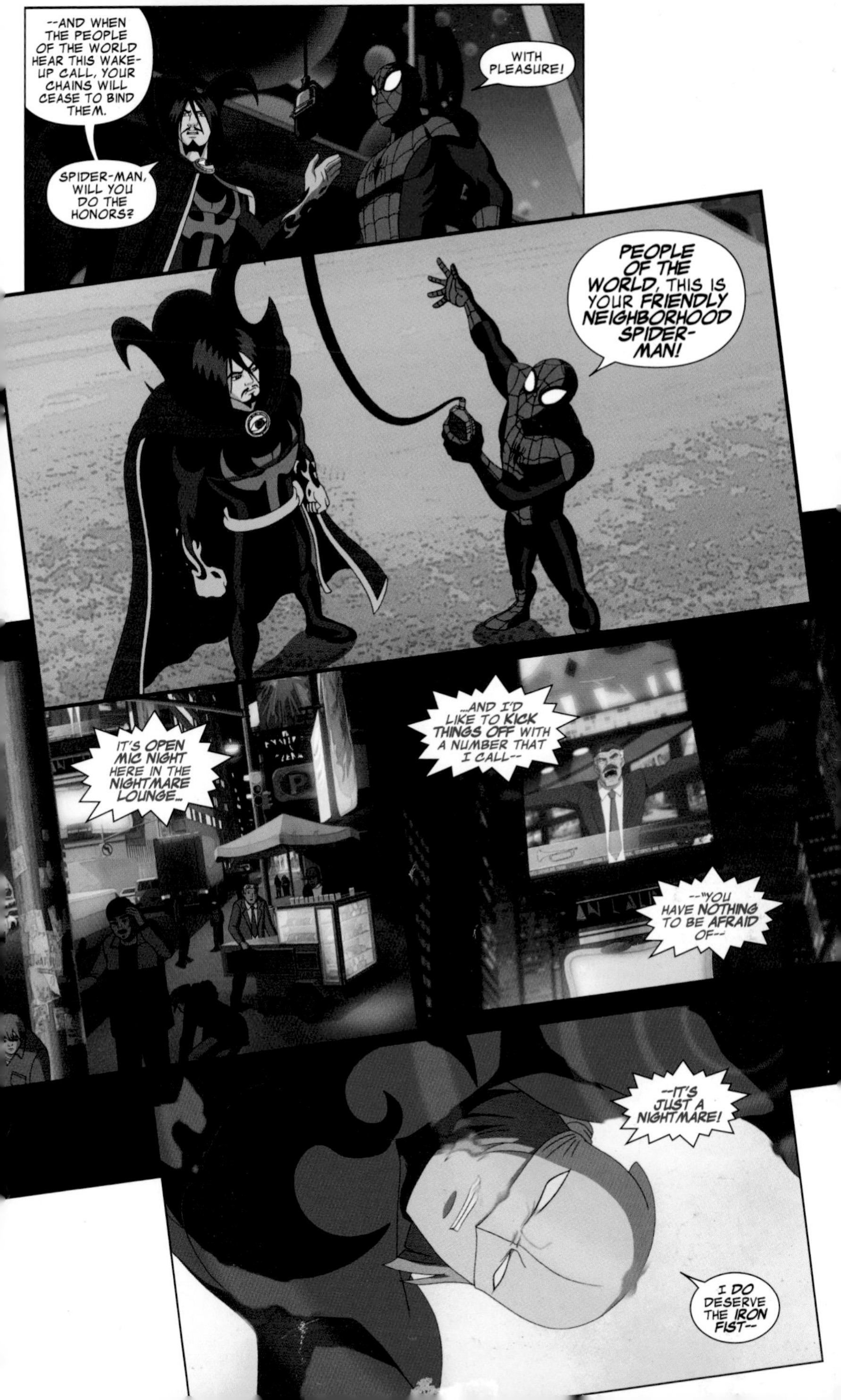
--AND WHEN THE PEOPLE OF THE WORLD HEAR THIS WAKE-UP CALL, YOUR CHAINS WILL CEASE TO BIND THEM.
SPIDER-MAN, WILL YOU DO THE HONORS?
WITH PLEASURE!
PEOPLE OF THE WORLD, THIS IS YOUR FRIENDLY NEIGHBORHOOD SPIDER-MAN!
IT'S OPEN MIC NIGHT HERE IN THE NIGHTMARE LOUNGE...
...AND I'D LIKE TO KICK THINGS OFF WITH A NUMBER THAT I CALL--
--"YOU HAVE NOTHING TO BE AFRAID OF--
--IT'S JUST A NIGHTMARE!
I DO DESERVE THE IRON FIST--

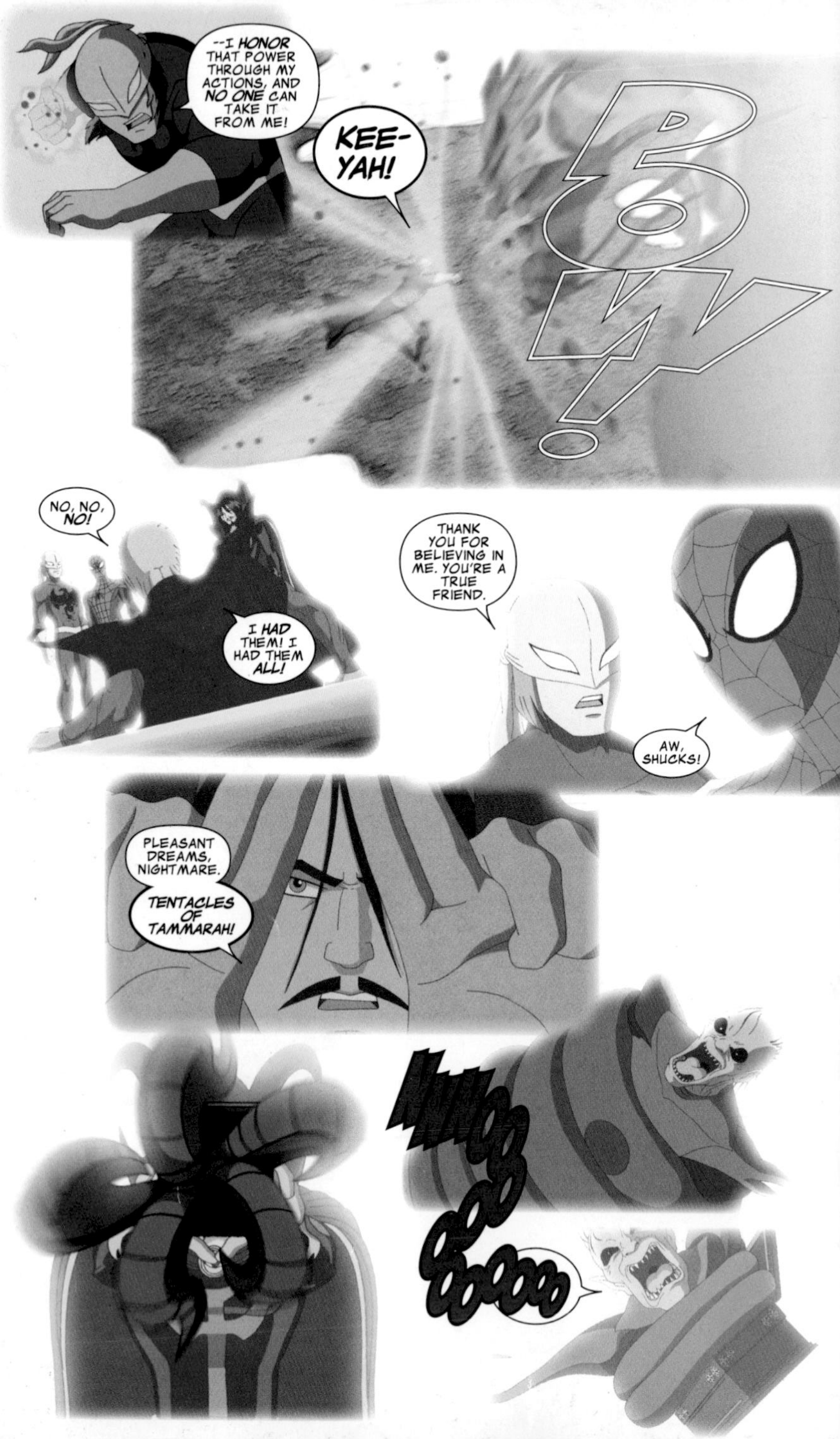
--I HONOR THAT POWER THROUGH MY ACTIONS, AND NO ONE CAN TAKE IT FROM ME!
KEE-YAH!
POW!
NO, NO, NO!
I HAD THEM! I HAD THEM ALL!
THANK YOU FOR BELIEVING IN ME. YOU'RE A TRUE FRIEND.
AW, SHUCKS!
PLEASANT DREAMS, NIGHTMARE.
TENTACLES OF TAMMARAH!
NNNOOOOOOOOOOO

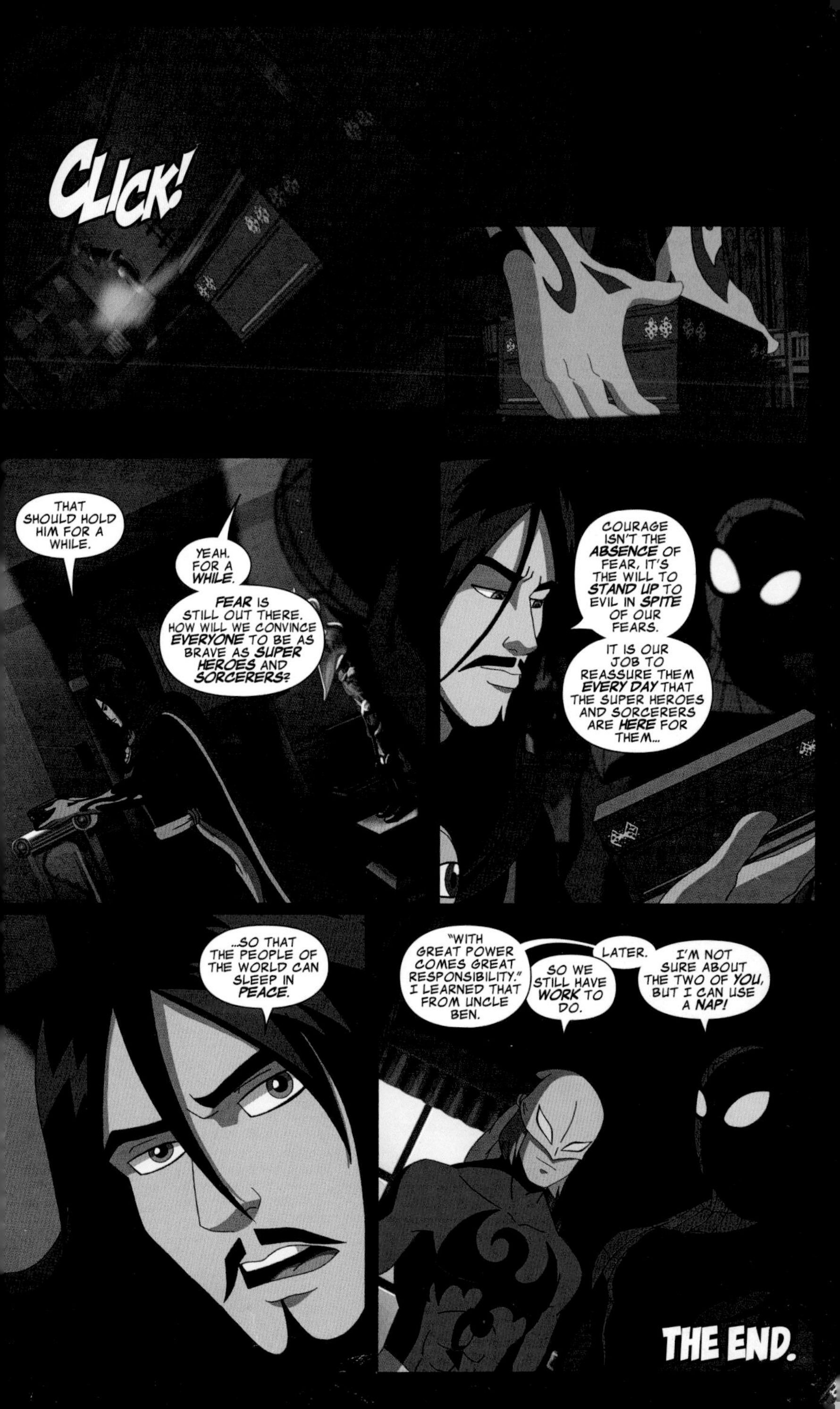
CLICK!
THAT SHOULD HOLD HIM FOR A WHILE.
YEAH. FOR A WHILE.
FEAR IS STILL OUT THERE. HOW WILL WE CONVINCE EVERYONE TO BE AS BRAVE AS SUPER HEROES AND SORCERERS?
COURAGE ISN'T THE ABSENCE OF FEAR, IT'S THE WILL TO STAND UP TO EVIL IN SPITE OF OUR FEARS.
IT IS OUR JOB TO REASSURE THEM EVERY DAY THAT THE SUPER HEROES AND SORCERERS ARE HERE FOR THEM...
...SO THAT THE PEOPLE OF THE WORLD CAN SLEEP IN PEACE.
"WITH GREAT POWER COMES GREAT RESPONSIBILITY." I LEARNED THAT FROM UNCLE BEN.
SO WE STILL HAVE WORK TO DO.
LATER.
I'M NOT SURE ABOUT THE TWO OF YOU, BUT I CAN USE A NAP!
THE END.

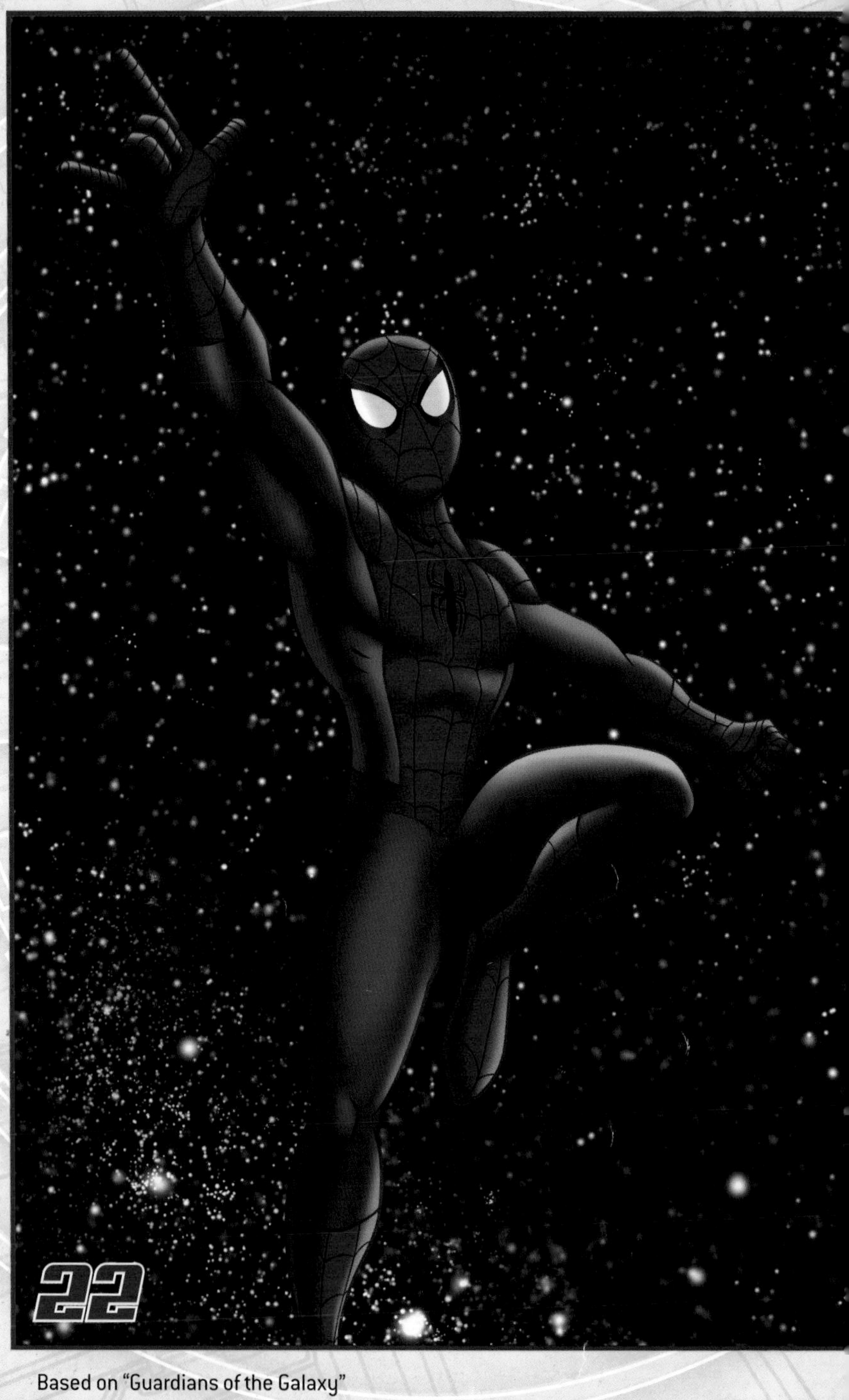
22

Based on "Guardians of the Galaxy"

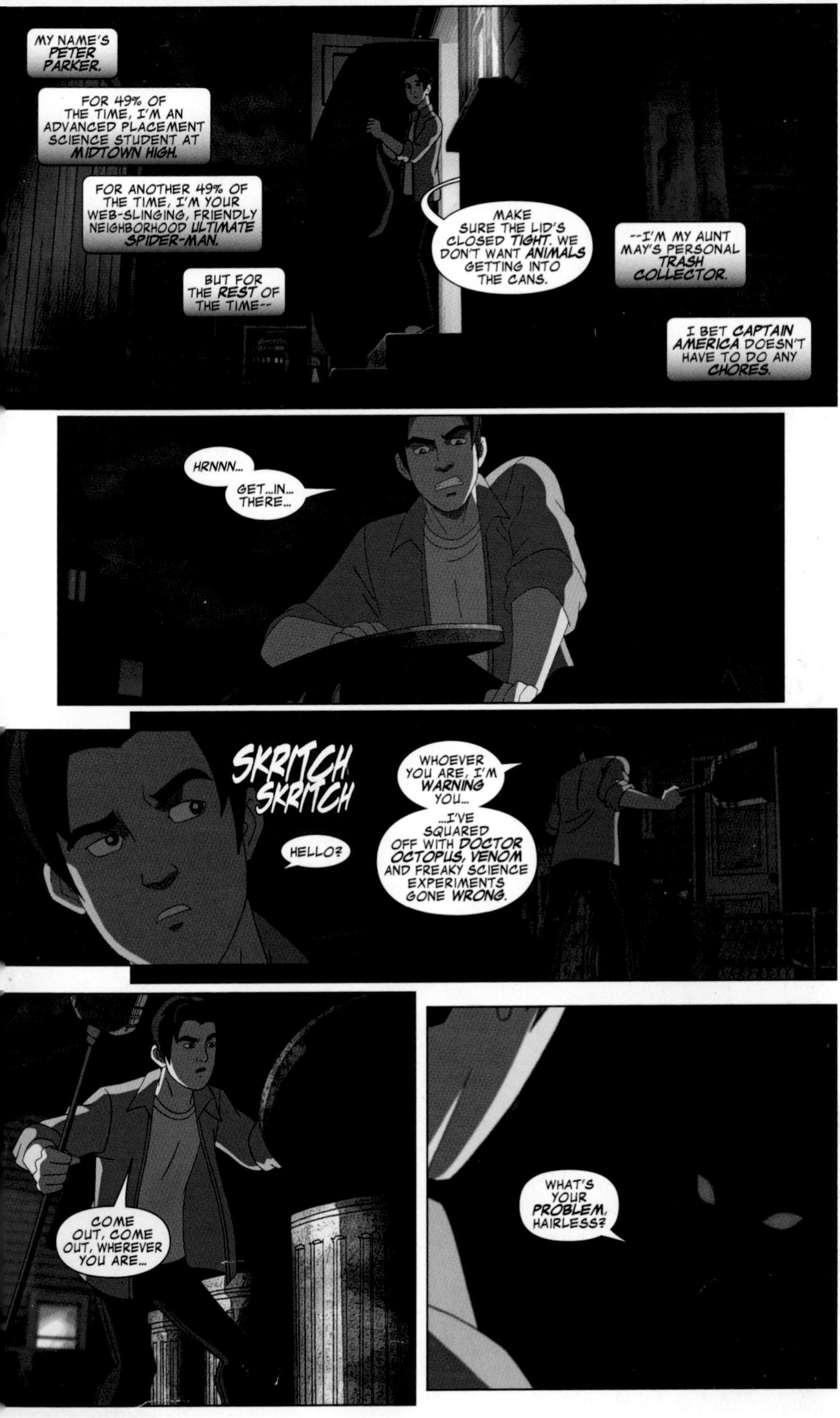

MY NAME'S PETER PARKER.
FOR 49% OF THE TIME, I'M AN ADVANCED PLACEMENT SCIENCE STUDENT AT MIDTOWN HIGH.
FOR ANOTHER 49% OF THE TIME, I'M YOUR WEB-SLINGING, FRIENDLY NEIGHBORHOOD ULTIMATE SPIDER-MAN.
BUT FOR THE REST OF THE TIME--
MAKE SURE THE LID'S CLOSED TIGHT. WE DON'T WANT ANIMALS GETTING INTO THE CANS.
--I'M MY AUNT MAY'S PERSONAL TRASH COLLECTOR.
I BET CAPTAIN AMERICA DOESN'T HAVE TO DO ANY CHORES.
HRNNN...
GET...IN... THERE...
SKRITCH SKRITCH
HELLO?
WHOEVER YOU ARE, I'M WARNING YOU...
...I'VE SQUARED OFF WITH DOCTOR OCTOPUS, VENOM AND FREAKY SCIENCE EXPERIMENTS GONE WRONG.
COME OUT, COME OUT, WHEREVER YOU ARE...
WHAT'S YOUR PROBLEM, HAIRLESS?

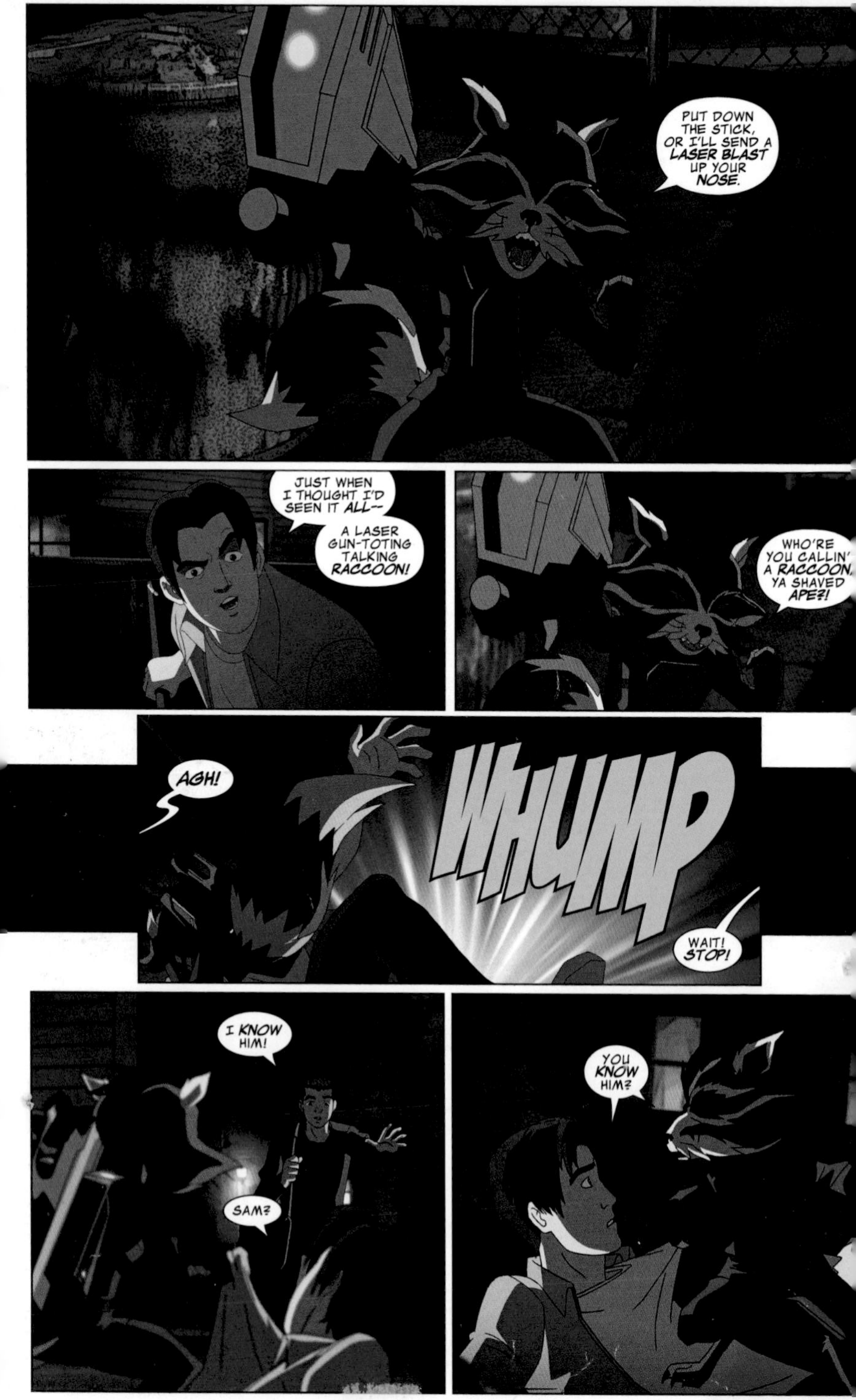
PUT DOWN THE STICK, OR I'LL SEND A LASER BLAST UP YOUR NOSE.
JUST WHEN I THOUGHT I'D SEEN IT ALL--
A LASER GUN-TOTING TALKING RACCOON!
WHO'RE YOU CALLIN' A RACCOON, YA SHAVED APE?!
AGH!
WHUMP
WAIT! STOP!
I KNOW HIM!
SAM?
YOU KNOW HIM?

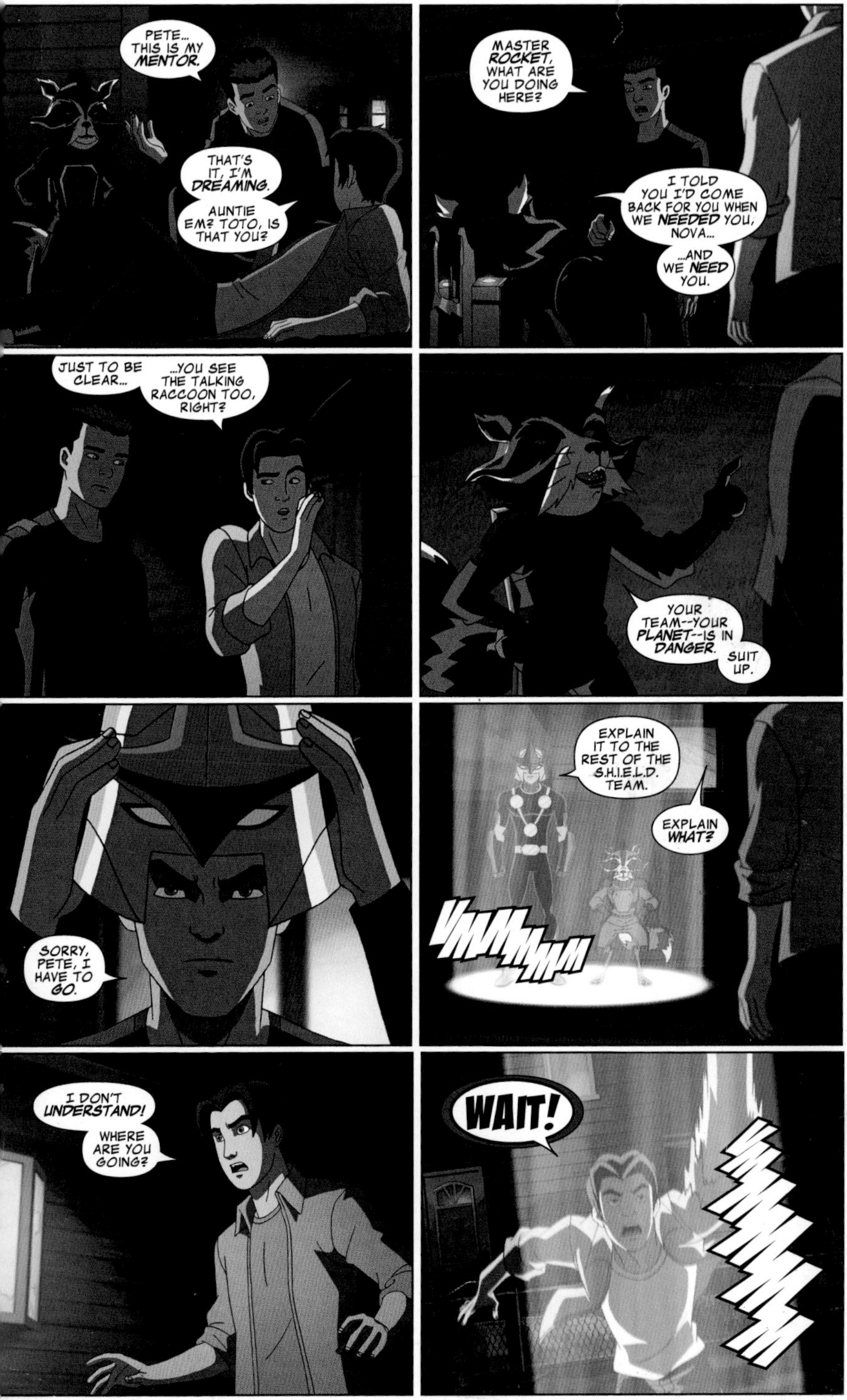
PETE... THIS IS MY MENTOR.
THAT'S IT, I'M DREAMING.
AUNTIE EM? TOTO, IS THAT YOU?
MASTER ROCKET, WHAT ARE YOU DOING HERE?
I TOLD YOU I'D COME BACK FOR YOU WHEN WE NEEDED YOU, NOVA...
...AND WE NEED YOU.
JUST TO BE CLEAR...
...YOU SEE THE TALKING RACCOON TOO, RIGHT?
YOUR TEAM--YOUR PLANET--IS IN DANGER.
SUIT UP.
SORRY, PETE, I HAVE TO GO.
EXPLAIN IT TO THE REST OF THE S.H.I.E.L.D. TEAM.
EXPLAIN WHAT?
I DON'T UNDERSTAND!
WHERE ARE YOU GOING?
WAIT!

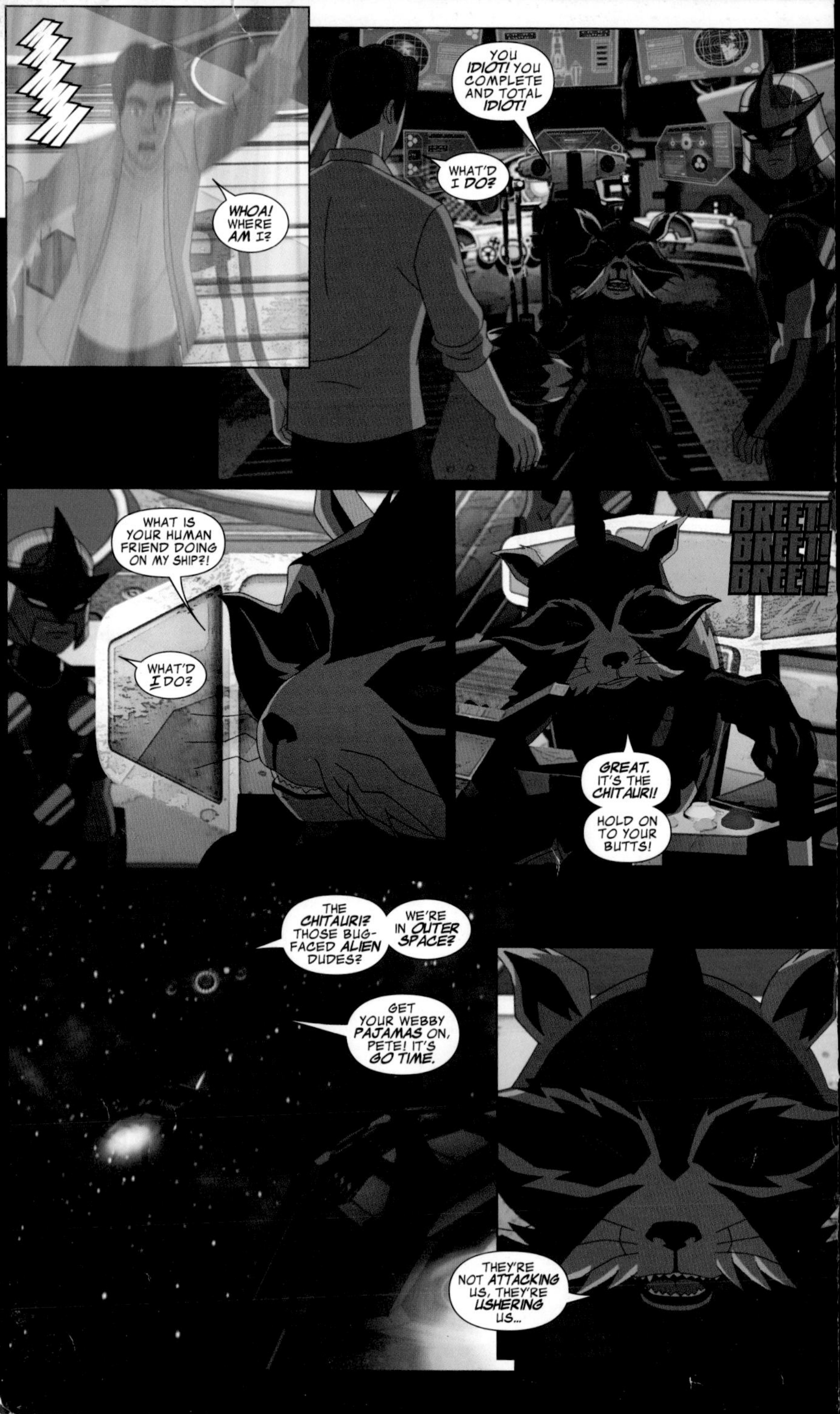

WHOA! WHERE AM I?
YOU IDIOT! YOU COMPLETE AND TOTAL IDIOT!
WHAT'D I DO?
WHAT IS YOUR HUMAN FRIEND DOING ON MY SHIP?!
WHAT'D I DO?
BREET! BREET! BREET!
GREAT. IT'S THE CHITAURI!
HOLD ON TO YOUR BUTTS!
THE CHITAURI? THOSE BUG-FACED ALIEN DUDES?
WE'RE IN OUTER SPACE?
GET YOUR WEBBY PAJAMAS ON, PETE! IT'S GO TIME.
THEY'RE NOT ATTACKING US, THEY'RE USHERING US...

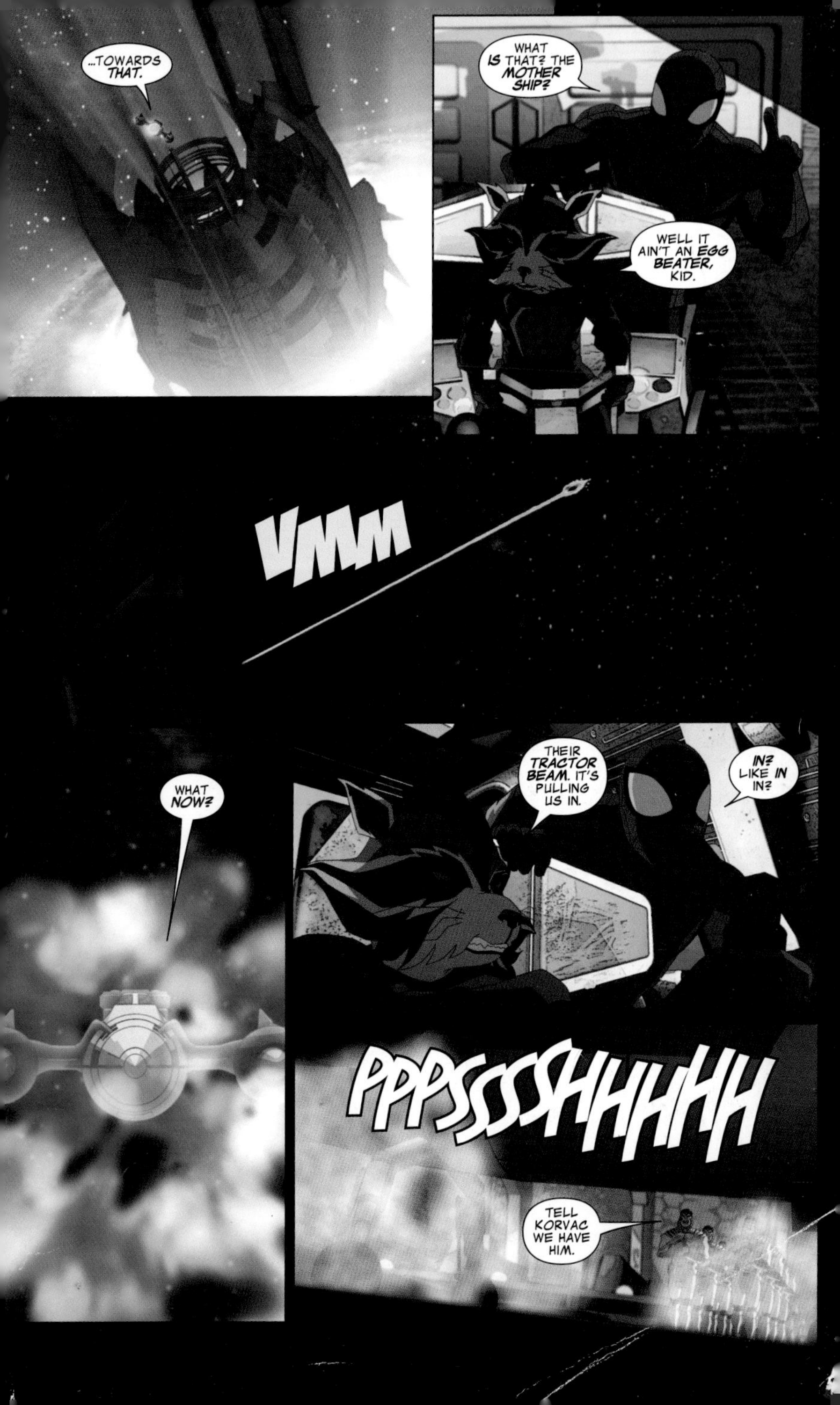
...TOWARDS THAT.
WHAT IS THAT? THE MOTHER SHIP?
WELL IT AIN'T AN EGG BEATER, KID.
VMM
WHAT NOW?
THEIR TRACTOR BEAM. IT'S PULLING US IN.
IN? LIKE IN IN?
PPPSSSSSHHHHHH
TELL KORVAC WE HAVE HIM.

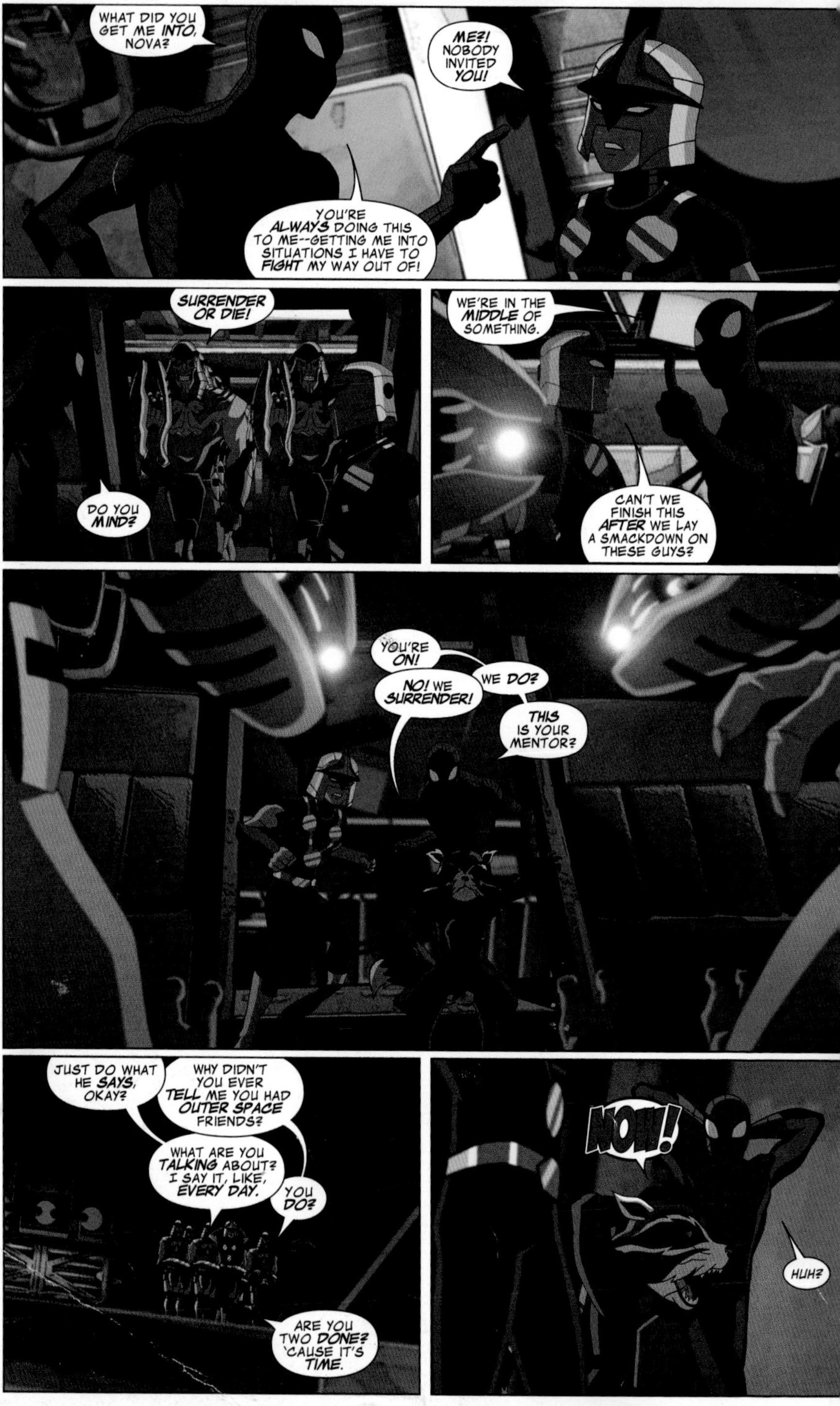

WHAT DID YOU GET ME INTO, NOVA?
ME?! NOBODY INVITED YOU!
YOU'RE ALWAYS DOING THIS TO ME--GETTING ME INTO SITUATIONS I HAVE TO FIGHT MY WAY OUT OF!
SURRENDER OR DIE!
DO YOU MIND?
WE'RE IN THE MIDDLE OF SOMETHING.
CAN'T WE FINISH THIS AFTER WE LAY A SMACKDOWN ON THESE GUYS?
YOU'RE ON!
NO! WE SURRENDER!
WE DO?
THIS IS YOUR MENTOR?
JUST DO WHAT HE SAYS, OKAY?
WHY DIDN'T YOU EVER TELL ME YOU HAD OUTER SPACE FRIENDS?
WHAT ARE YOU TALKING ABOUT? I SAY IT, LIKE, EVERY DAY.
YOU DO?
ARE YOU TWO DONE? 'CAUSE IT'S TIME.
NOW!
HUH?

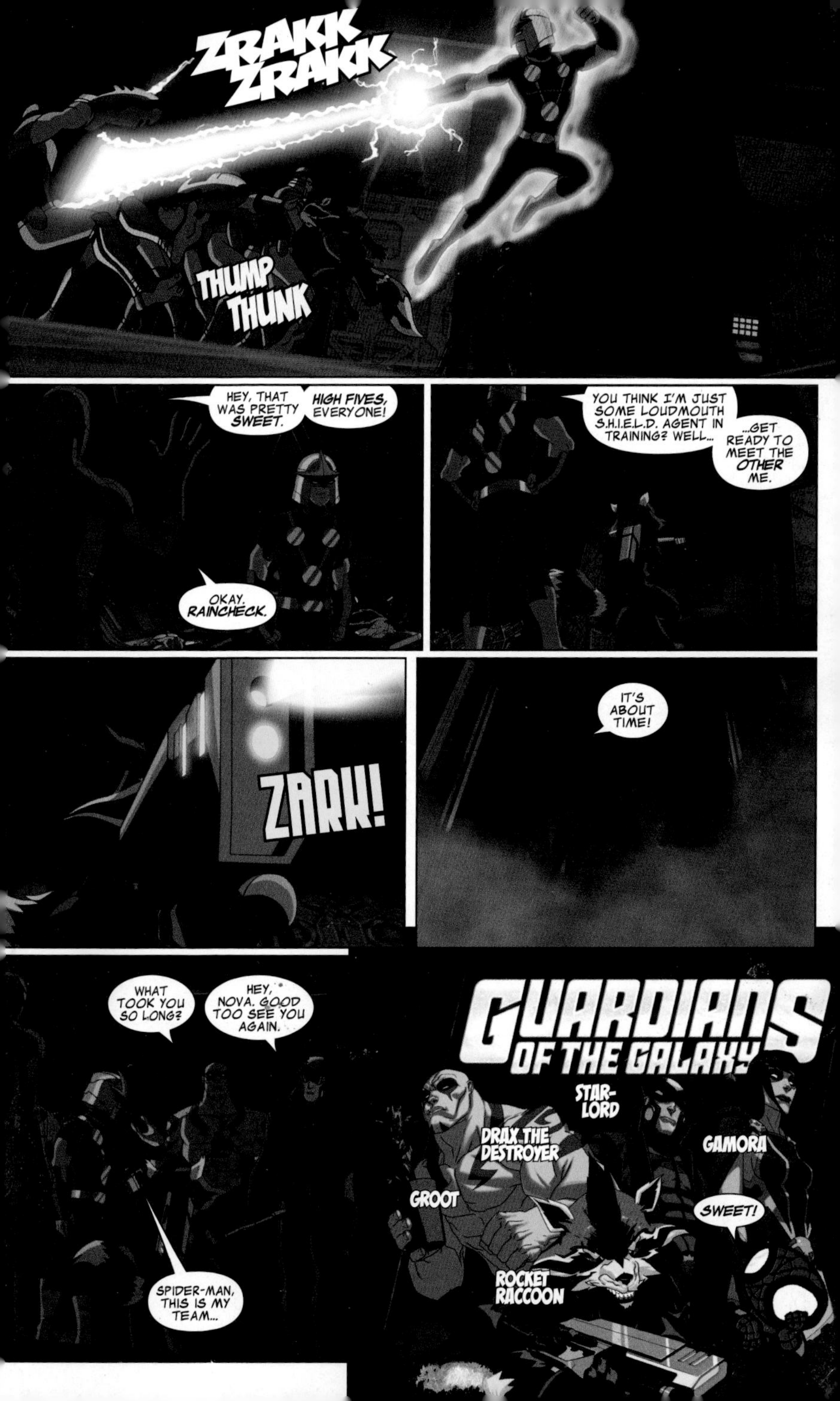
ZRAKK ZRAKK
THUMP THUNK
HEY, THAT WAS PRETTY SWEET.
HIGH FIVES, EVERYONE!
OKAY. RAINCHECK.
YOU THINK I'M JUST SOME LOUDMOUTH S.H.I.E.L.D. AGENT IN TRAINING? WELL...
...GET READY TO MEET THE OTHER ME.
ZARK!
IT'S ABOUT TIME!
WHAT TOOK YOU SO LONG?
HEY, NOVA. GOOD TOO SEE YOU AGAIN.
GUARDIANS OF THE GALAXY
STAR-LORD
DRAX THE DESTROYER
GAMORA
GROOT
SWEET!
ROCKET RACCOON
SPIDER-MAN, THIS IS MY TEAM...

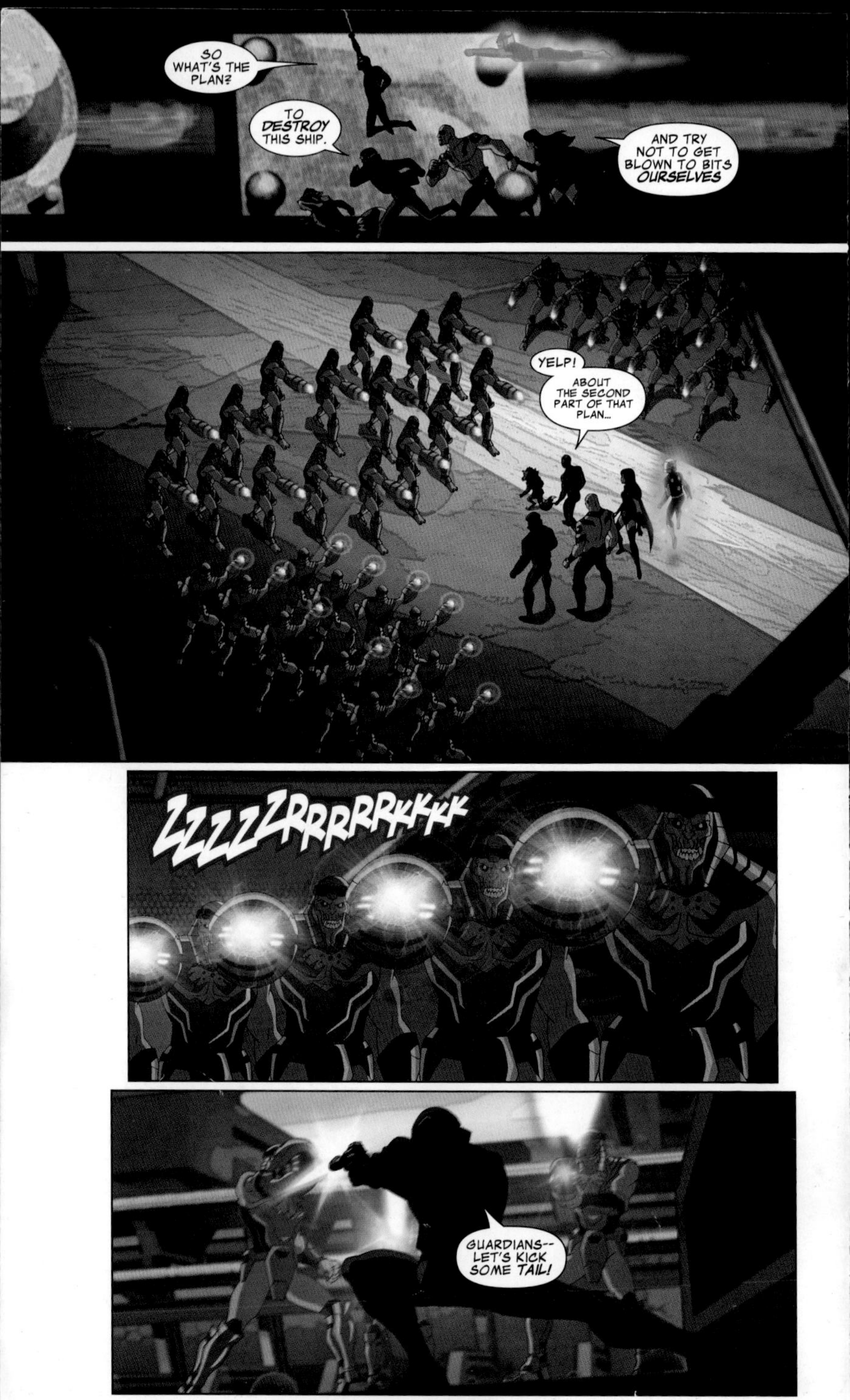
SO WHAT'S THE PLAN?
TO DESTROY THIS SHIP.
AND TRY NOT TO GET BLOWN TO BITS OURSELVES
YELP!
ABOUT THE SECOND PART OF THAT PLAN...
ZZZZZRRRRRKKKK
GUARDIANS-- LET'S KICK SOME TAIL!

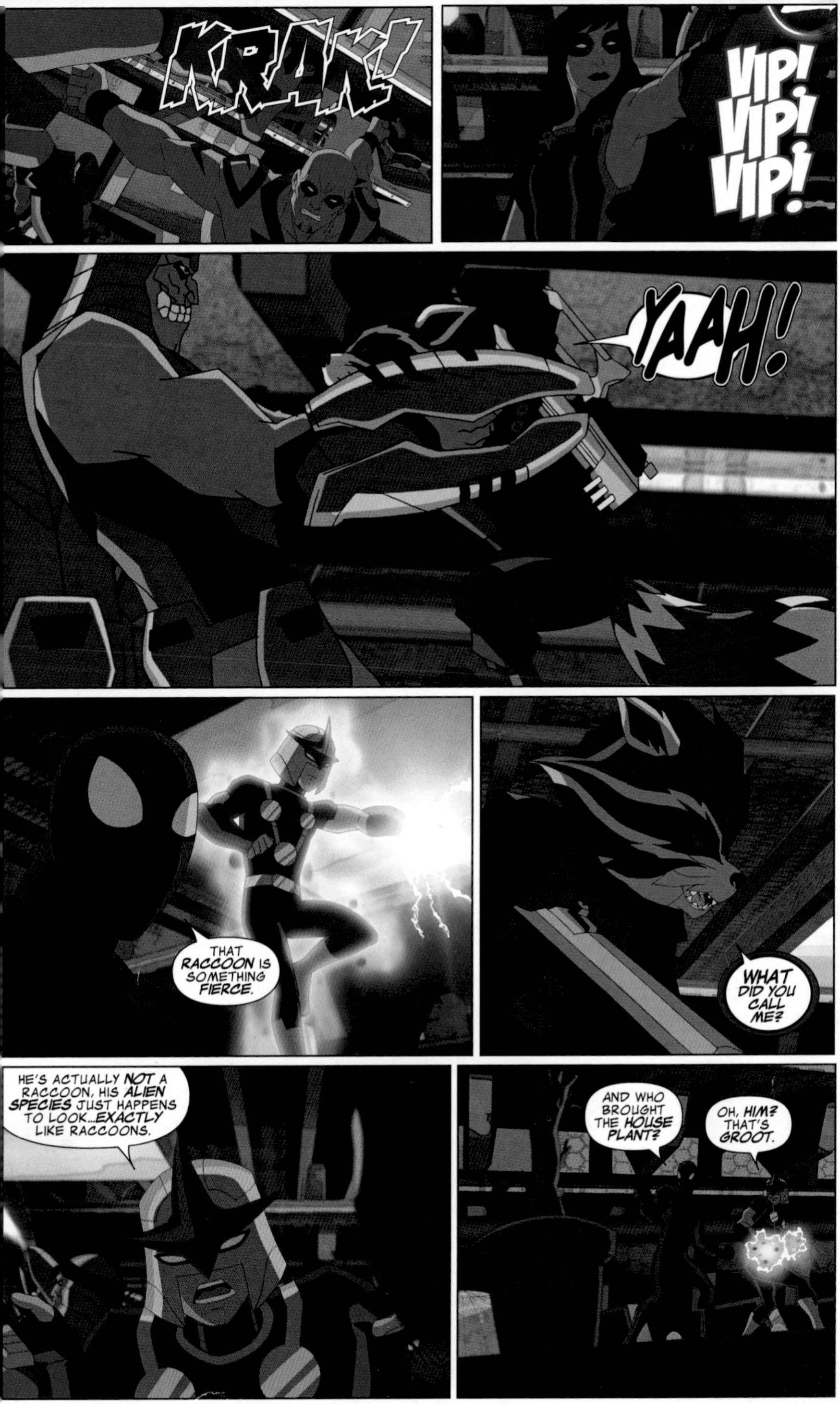
KRAK!
VIP! VIP! VIP!
YAAH!
THAT RACCOON IS SOMETHING FIERCE.
WHAT DID YOU CALL ME?
HE'S ACTUALLY NOT A RACCOON, HIS ALIEN SPECIES JUST HAPPENS TO LOOK...EXACTLY LIKE RACCOONS.
AND WHO BROUGHT THE HOUSE PLANT?
OH, HIM? THAT'S GROOT.

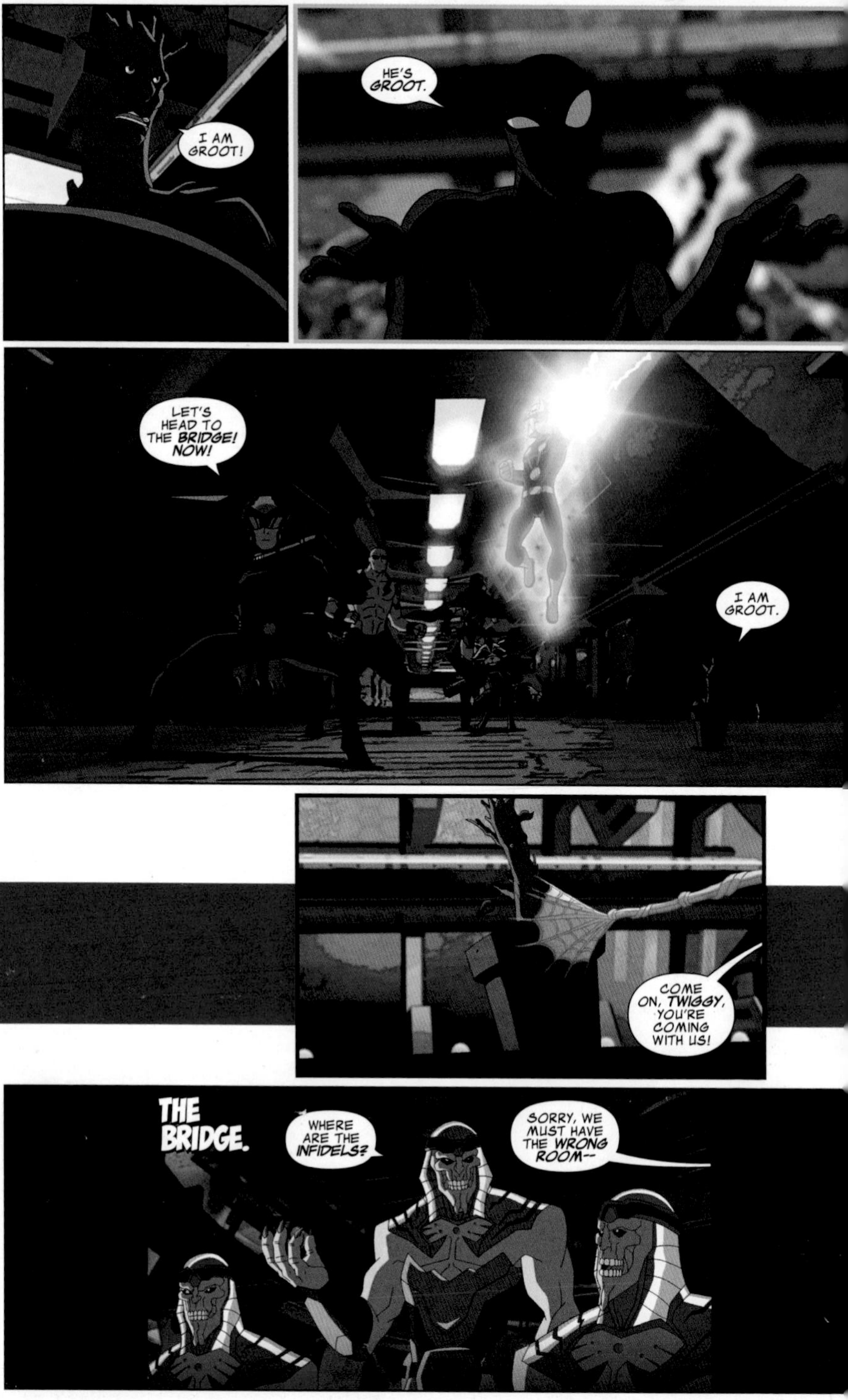
I AM GROOT!
HE'S GROOT.
LET'S HEAD TO THE BRIDGE! NOW!
I AM GROOT.
COME ON, TWIGGY, YOU'RE COMING WITH US!
THE BRIDGE.
WHERE ARE THE INFIDELS?
SORRY, WE MUST HAVE THE WRONG ROOM--

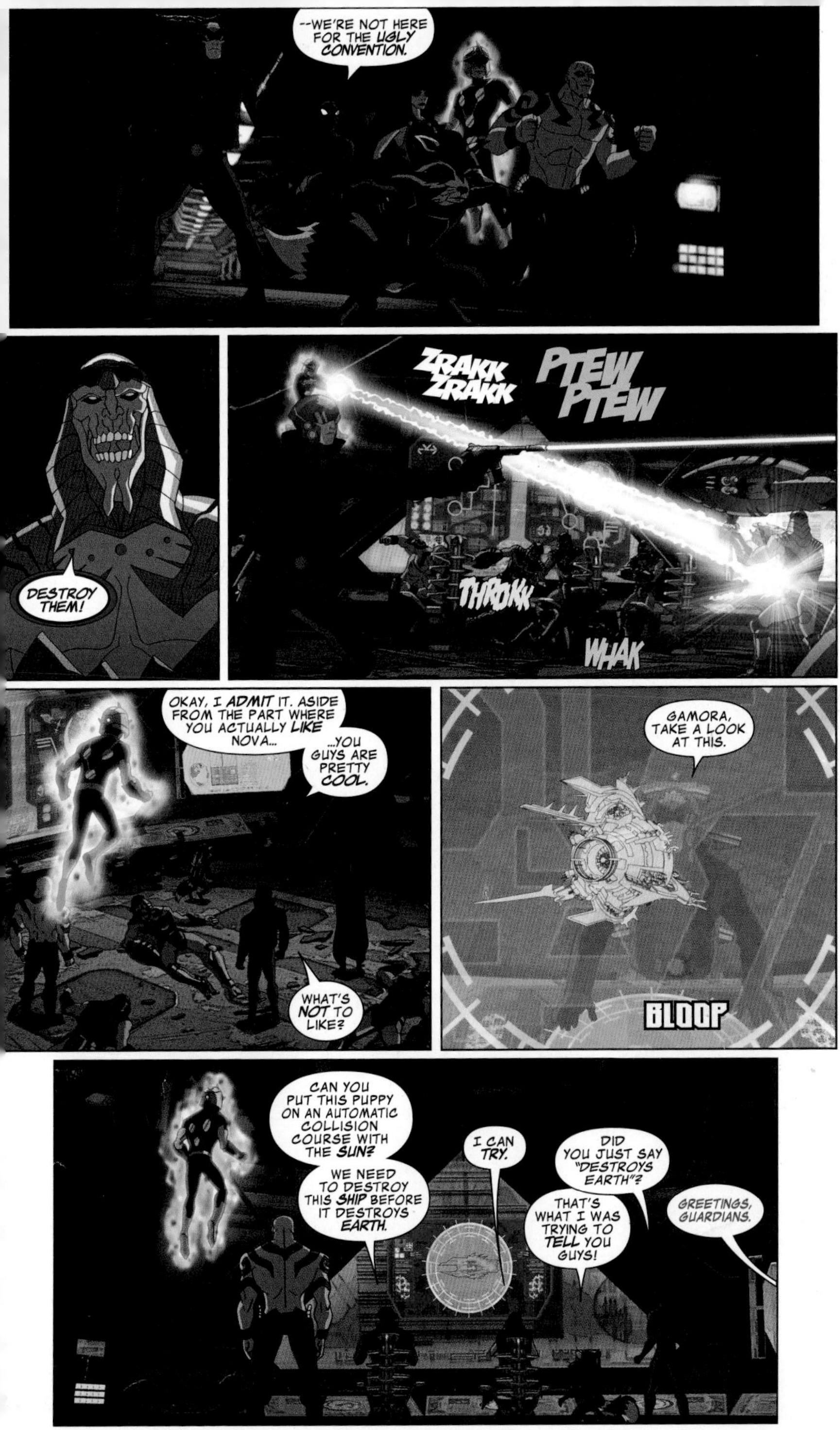

--WE'RE NOT HERE FOR THE UGLY CONVENTION.
DESTROY THEM!
ZRAKK ZRAKK
PTEW PTEW
THROKK
WHAK
OKAY, I ADMIT IT. ASIDE FROM THE PART WHERE YOU ACTUALLY LIKE NOVA...
...YOU GUYS ARE PRETTY COOL.
WHAT'S NOT TO LIKE?
GAMORA, TAKE A LOOK AT THIS.
BLOOP
CAN YOU PUT THIS PUPPY ON AN AUTOMATIC COLLISION COURSE WITH THE SUN?
WE NEED TO DESTROY THIS SHIP BEFORE IT DESTROYS EARTH.
I CAN TRY.
DID YOU JUST SAY "DESTROYS EARTH"?
THAT'S WHAT I WAS TRYING TO TELL YOU GUYS!
GREETINGS, GUARDIANS.

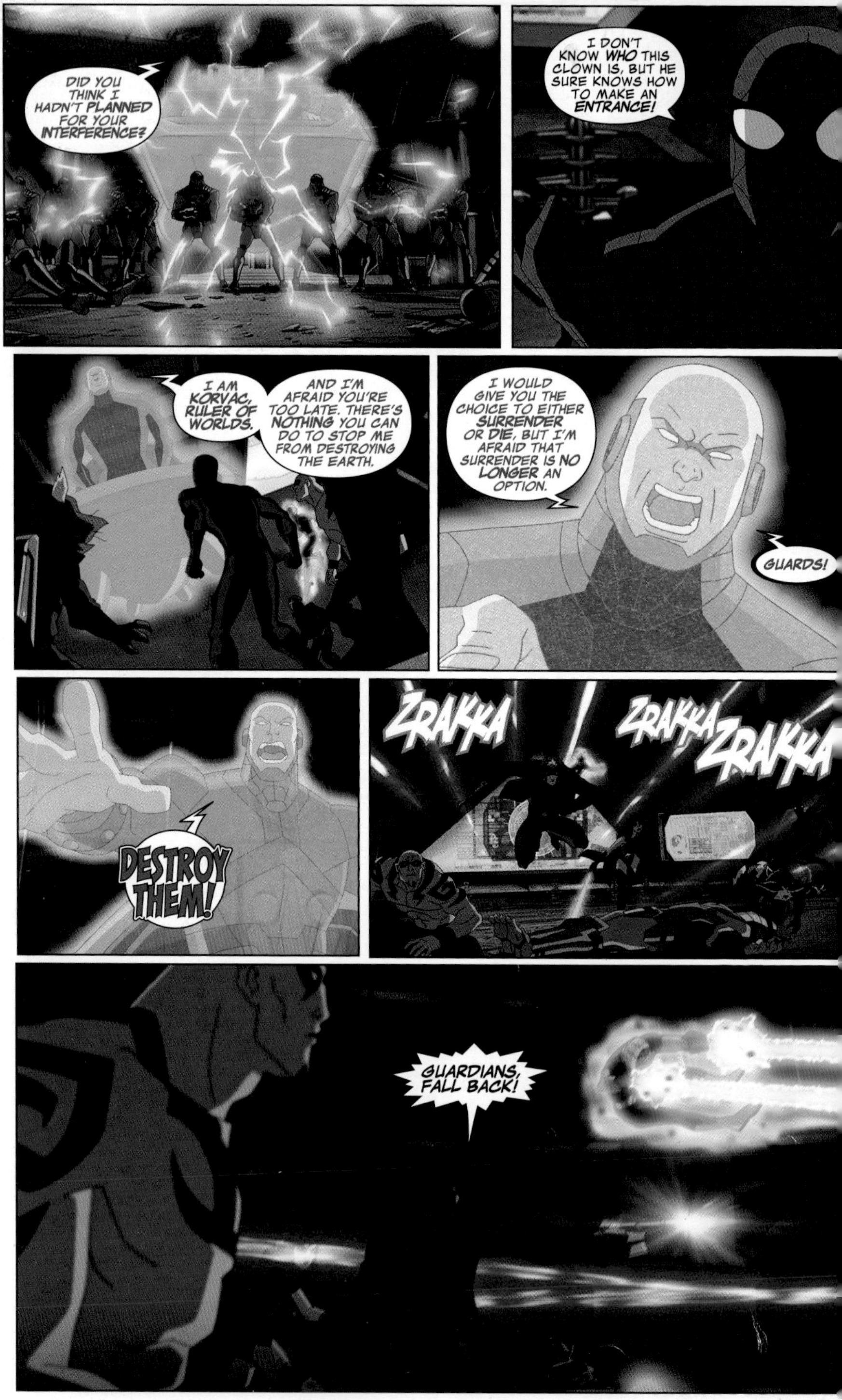
DID YOU THINK I HADN'T PLANNED FOR YOUR INTERFERENCE?
I DON'T KNOW WHO THIS CLOWN IS, BUT HE SURE KNOWS HOW TO MAKE AN ENTRANCE!
I AM KORVAC, RULER OF WORLDS.
AND I'M AFRAID YOU'RE TOO LATE. THERE'S NOTHING YOU CAN DO TO STOP ME FROM DESTROYING THE EARTH.
I WOULD GIVE YOU THE CHOICE TO EITHER SURRENDER OR DIE, BUT I'M AFRAID THAT SURRENDER IS NO LONGER AN OPTION.
GUARDS!
DESTROY THEM!
ZRAKKA
ZRAKKA ZRAKKA
GUARDIANS, FALL BACK!

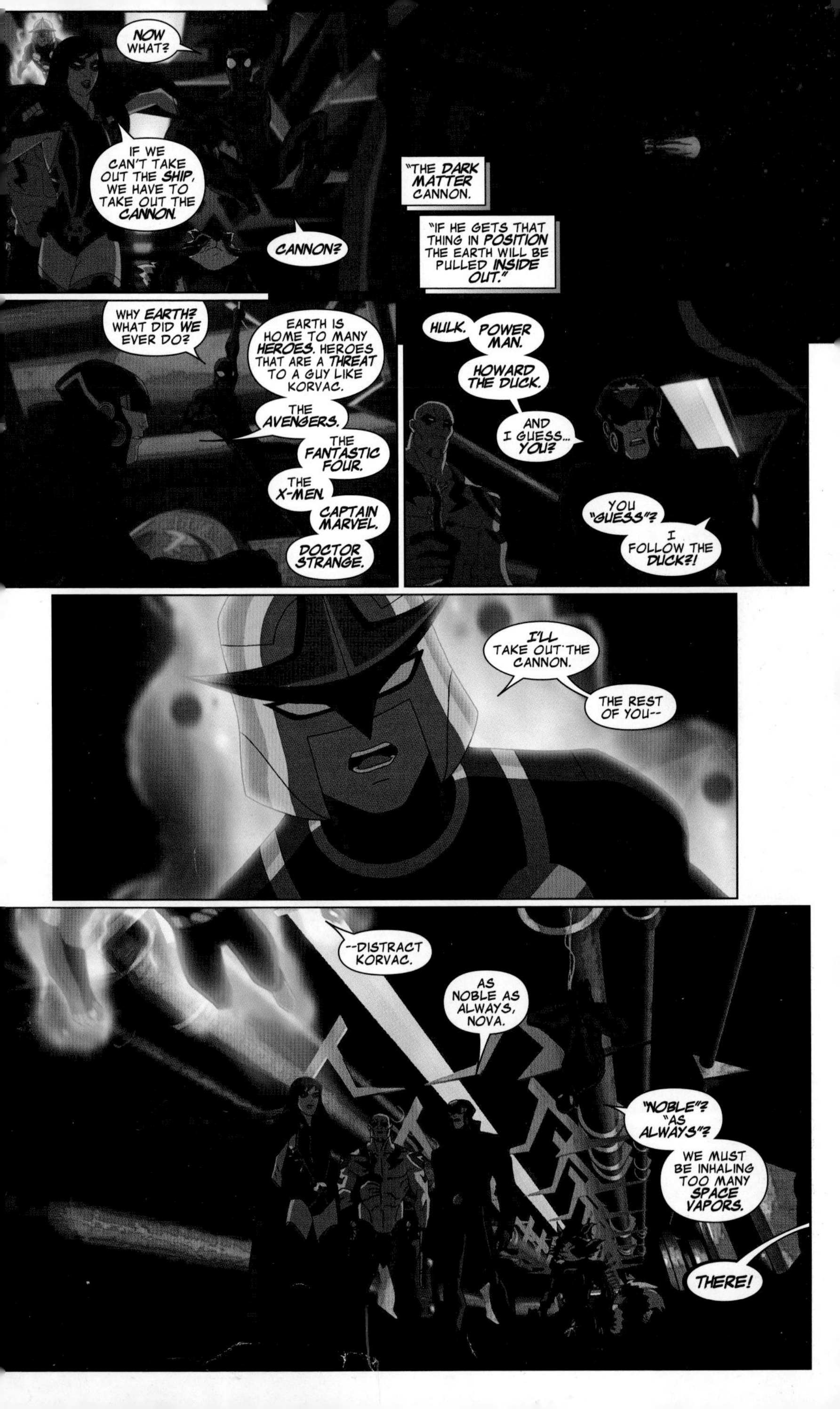

NOW WHAT?
IF WE CAN'T TAKE OUT THE SHIP, WE HAVE TO TAKE OUT THE CANNON.
CANNON?
"THE DARK MATTER CANNON.
"IF HE GETS THAT THING IN POSITION THE EARTH WILL BE PULLED INSIDE OUT."
WHY EARTH? WHAT DID WE EVER DO?
EARTH IS HOME TO MANY HEROES. HEROES THAT ARE A THREAT TO A GUY LIKE KORVAC.
THE AVENGERS.
THE FANTASTIC FOUR.
THE X-MEN.
CAPTAIN MARVEL.
DOCTOR STRANGE.
HULK.
POWER MAN.
HOWARD THE DUCK.
AND I GUESS... YOU?
YOU "GUESS"?
I FOLLOW THE DUCK?!
I'LL TAKE OUT THE CANNON.
THE REST OF YOU--
--DISTRACT KORVAC.
AS NOBLE AS ALWAYS, NOVA.
"NOBLE"? "AS ALWAYS"?
WE MUST BE INHALING TOO MANY SPACE VAPORS.
THERE!

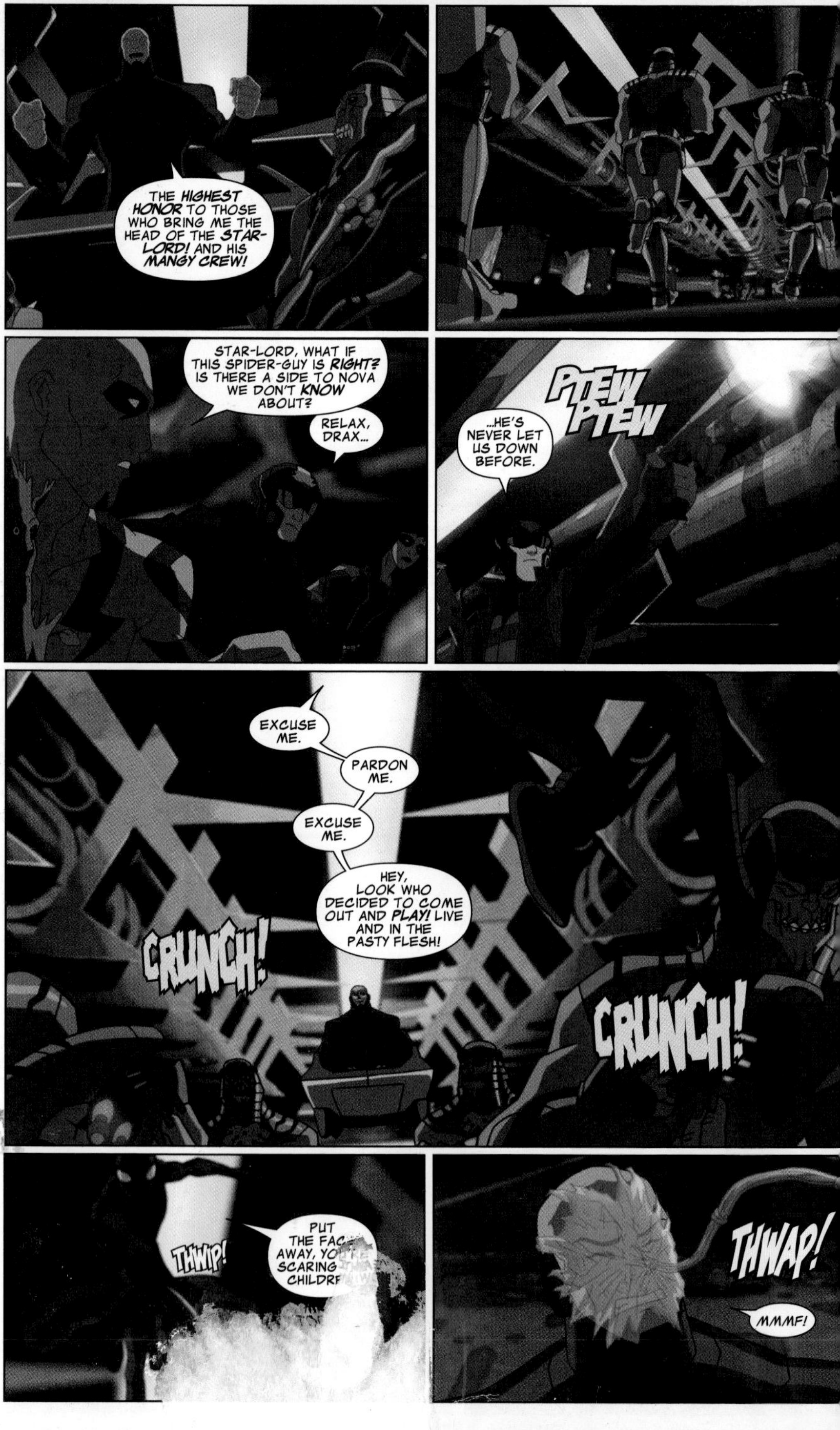

THE HIGHEST HONOR TO THOSE WHO BRING ME THE HEAD OF THE STAR-LORD! AND HIS MANGY CREW!
STAR-LORD, WHAT IF THIS SPIDER-GUY IS RIGHT? IS THERE A SIDE TO NOVA WE DON'T KNOW ABOUT?
RELAX, DRAX...
PTEW PTEW
...HE'S NEVER LET US DOWN BEFORE.
EXCUSE ME.
PARDON ME.
EXCUSE ME.
HEY, LOOK WHO DECIDED TO COME OUT AND PLAY! LIVE AND IN THE PASTY FLESH!
CRUNCH!
CRUNCH!
THWIP!
PUT THE FAC AWAY, YO SCARING CHILDR
THWAP!
MMMF!

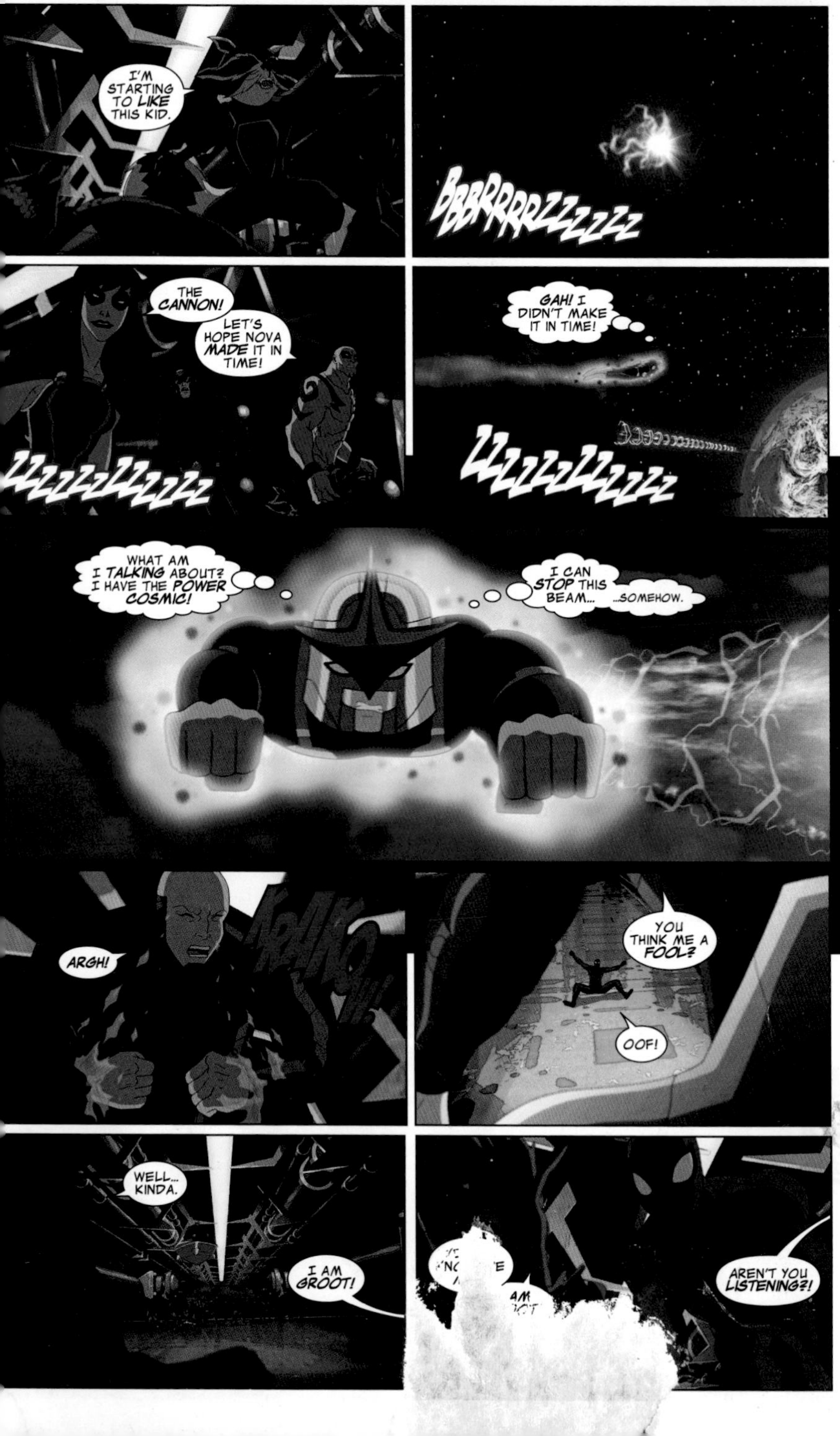
I'M STARTING TO LIKE THIS KID.
BBBRRRRRZZZZZZZ
THE CANNON!
LET'S HOPE NOVA MADE IT IN TIME!
ZZZZZZZZZZZZZZ
GAH! I DIDN'T MAKE IT IN TIME!
ZZZZZZZZZZZZZZ
WHAT AM I TALKING ABOUT? I HAVE THE POWER COSMIC!
I CAN STOP THIS BEAM...
...SOMEHOW.
ARGH!
YOU THINK ME A FOOL?
OOF!
WELL... KINDA.
I AM GROOT!
AREN'T YOU LISTENING?!

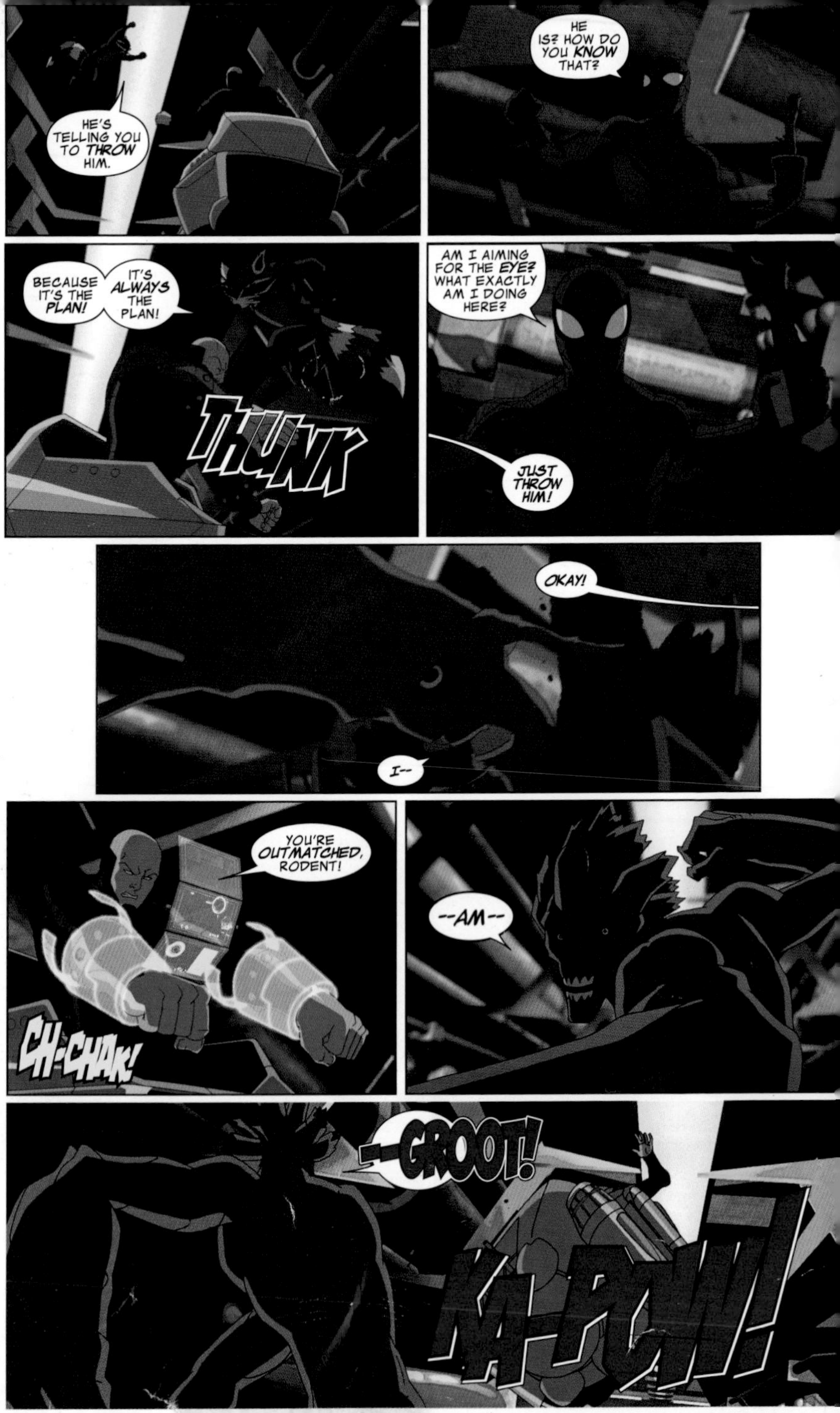

HE'S TELLING YOU TO THROW HIM.
HE IS? HOW DO YOU KNOW THAT?
BECAUSE IT'S THE PLAN!
IT'S ALWAYS THE PLAN!
THUNK
AM I AIMING FOR THE EYE? WHAT EXACTLY AM I DOING HERE?
JUST THROW HIM!
OKAY!
I--
YOU'RE OUTMATCHED, RODENT!
CH-CHAK!
--AM--
--GROOT!
KA-POW!

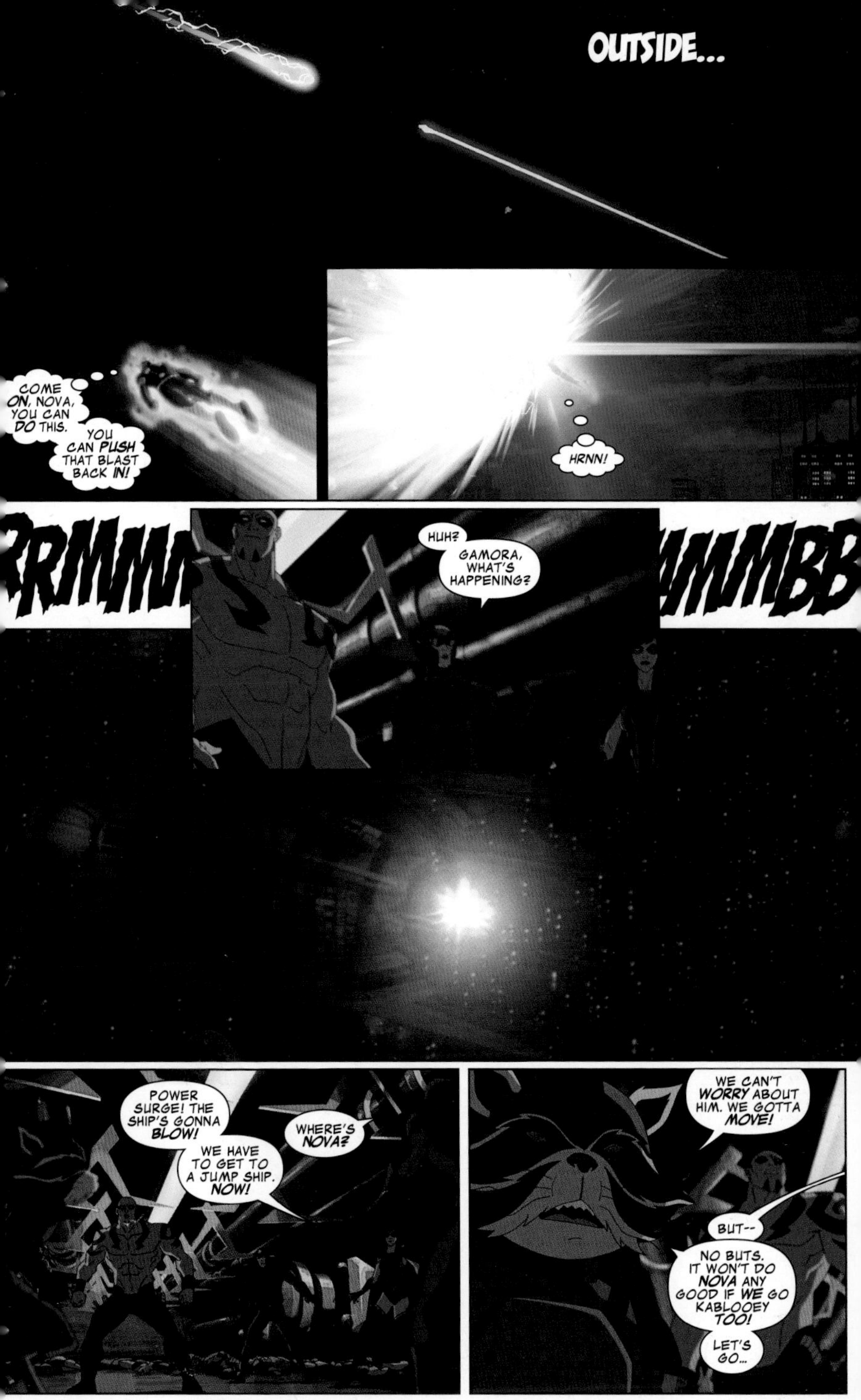

OUTSIDE...
COME ON, NOVA, YOU CAN DO THIS.
YOU CAN PUSH THAT BLAST BACK IN!
HRNN!
HUH? GAMORA, WHAT'S HAPPENING?
POWER SURGE! THE SHIP'S GONNA BLOW!
WE HAVE TO GET TO A JUMP SHIP. NOW!
WHERE'S NOVA?
WE CAN'T WORRY ABOUT HIM. WE GOTTA MOVE!
BUT--
NO BUTS. IT WON'T DO NOVA ANY GOOD IF WE GO KABLOOEY TOO!
LET'S GO...

...AND PRAY THAT THE KID'S ALL RIGHT.

EVERYONE ACCOUNTED FOR?

YEAH, STAR-LORD. ALL EXCEPT FOR *NOVA*.

WE'LL FIND HIM.

I'M SURE HE'S ALL RIGHT. HE'S *NOVA*, AFTER ALL.

COME ON, NOVA, DON'T MAKE A LIAR OUT OF ME.

THERE HE IS!

SAM!

DON'T JUST *STAND* THERE, KID...

"LET'S GO GET HIM!"

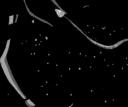

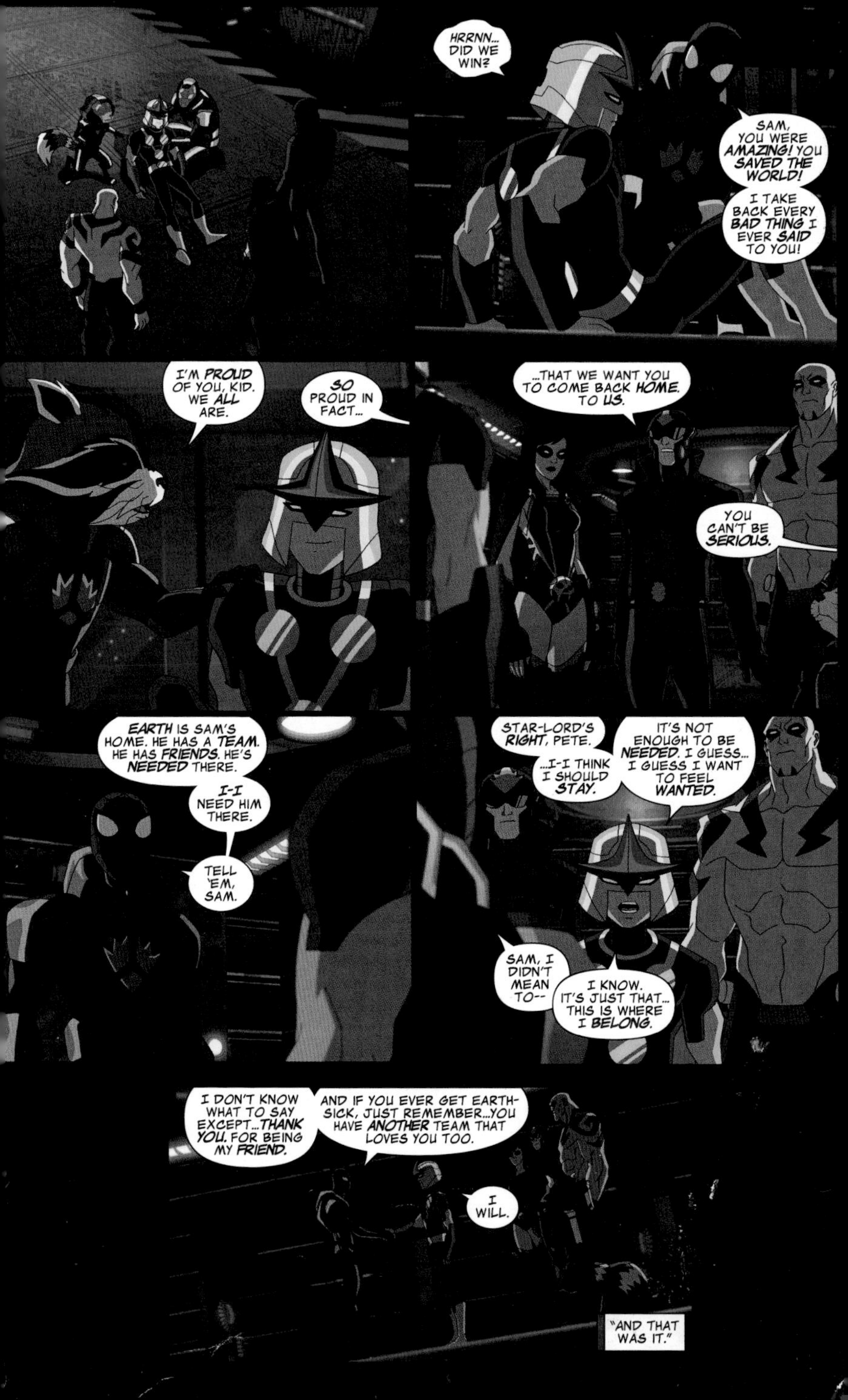
HRRNN... DID WE WIN?
SAM, YOU WERE AMAZING! YOU SAVED THE WORLD!
I TAKE BACK EVERY BAD THING I EVER SAID TO YOU!
I'M PROUD OF YOU, KID. WE ALL ARE.
SO PROUD IN FACT...
...THAT WE WANT YOU TO COME BACK HOME. TO US.
YOU CAN'T BE SERIOUS.
EARTH IS SAM'S HOME. HE HAS A TEAM. HE HAS FRIENDS. HE'S NEEDED THERE.
I-I NEED HIM THERE.
TELL 'EM, SAM.
STAR-LORD'S RIGHT, PETE.
...I-I THINK I SHOULD STAY.
IT'S NOT ENOUGH TO BE NEEDED, I GUESS... I GUESS I WANT TO FEEL WANTED.
SAM, I DIDN'T MEAN TO--
I KNOW. IT'S JUST THAT... THIS IS WHERE I BELONG.
I DON'T KNOW WHAT TO SAY EXCEPT...THANK YOU. FOR BEING MY FRIEND.
AND IF YOU EVER GET EARTH-SICK, JUST REMEMBER...YOU HAVE ANOTHER TEAM THAT LOVES YOU TOO.
I WILL.
"AND THAT WAS IT."

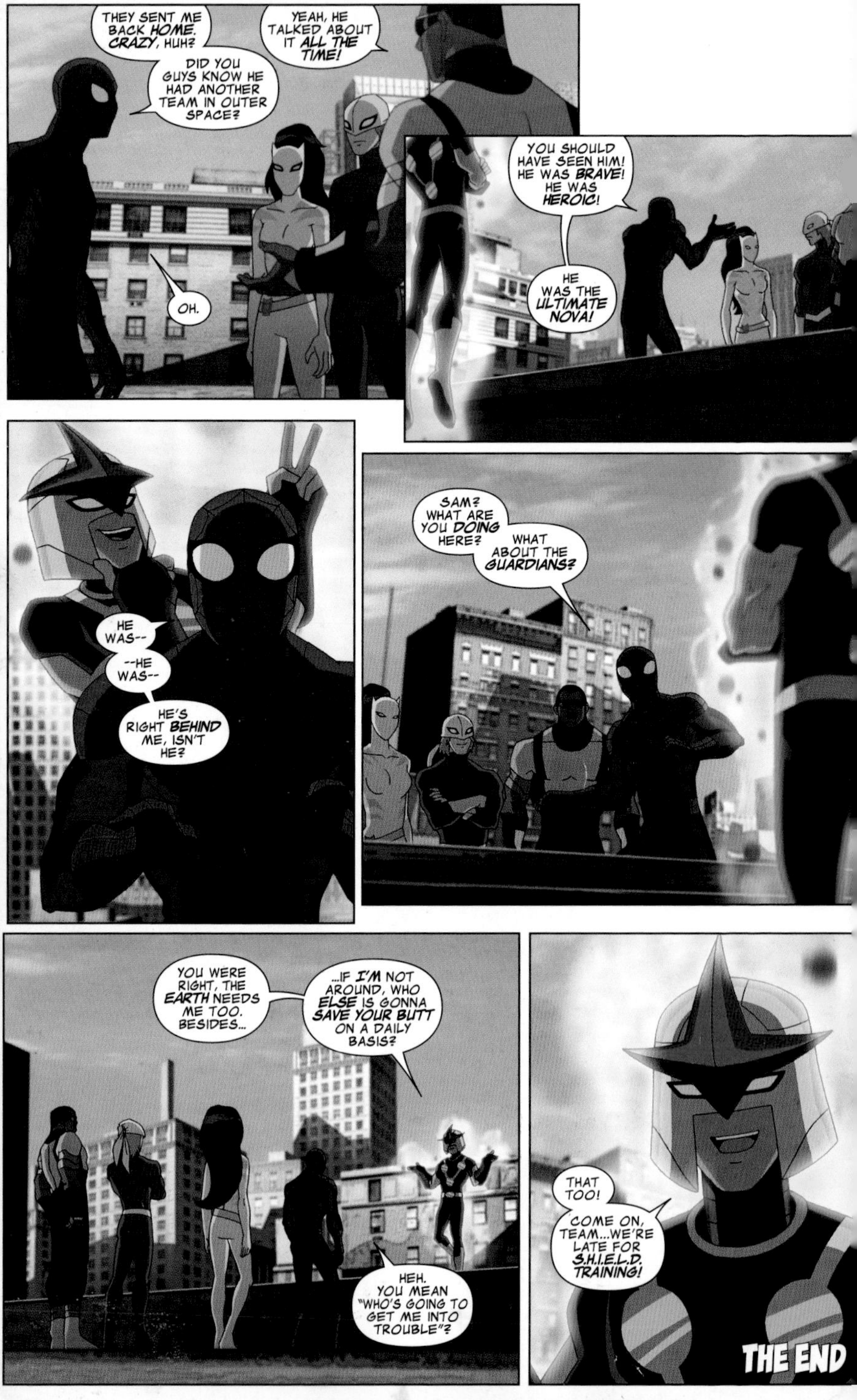
THEY SENT ME BACK HOME. CRAZY, HUH?
DID YOU GUYS KNOW HE HAD ANOTHER TEAM IN OUTER SPACE?
YEAH, HE TALKED ABOUT IT ALL THE TIME!
OH.
YOU SHOULD HAVE SEEN HIM! HE WAS BRAVE! HE WAS HEROIC!
HE WAS THE ULTIMATE NOVA!
HE WAS--
--HE WAS--
HE'S RIGHT BEHIND ME, ISN'T HE?
SAM? WHAT ARE YOU DOING HERE?
WHAT ABOUT THE GUARDIANS?
YOU WERE RIGHT, THE EARTH NEEDS ME TOO. BESIDES...
...IF I'M NOT AROUND, WHO ELSE IS GONNA SAVE YOUR BUTT ON A DAILY BASIS?
HEH. YOU MEAN "WHO'S GOING TO GET ME INTO TROUBLE"?
THAT TOO!
COME ON, TEAM...WE'RE LATE FOR S.H.I.E.L.D. TRAINING!
THE END

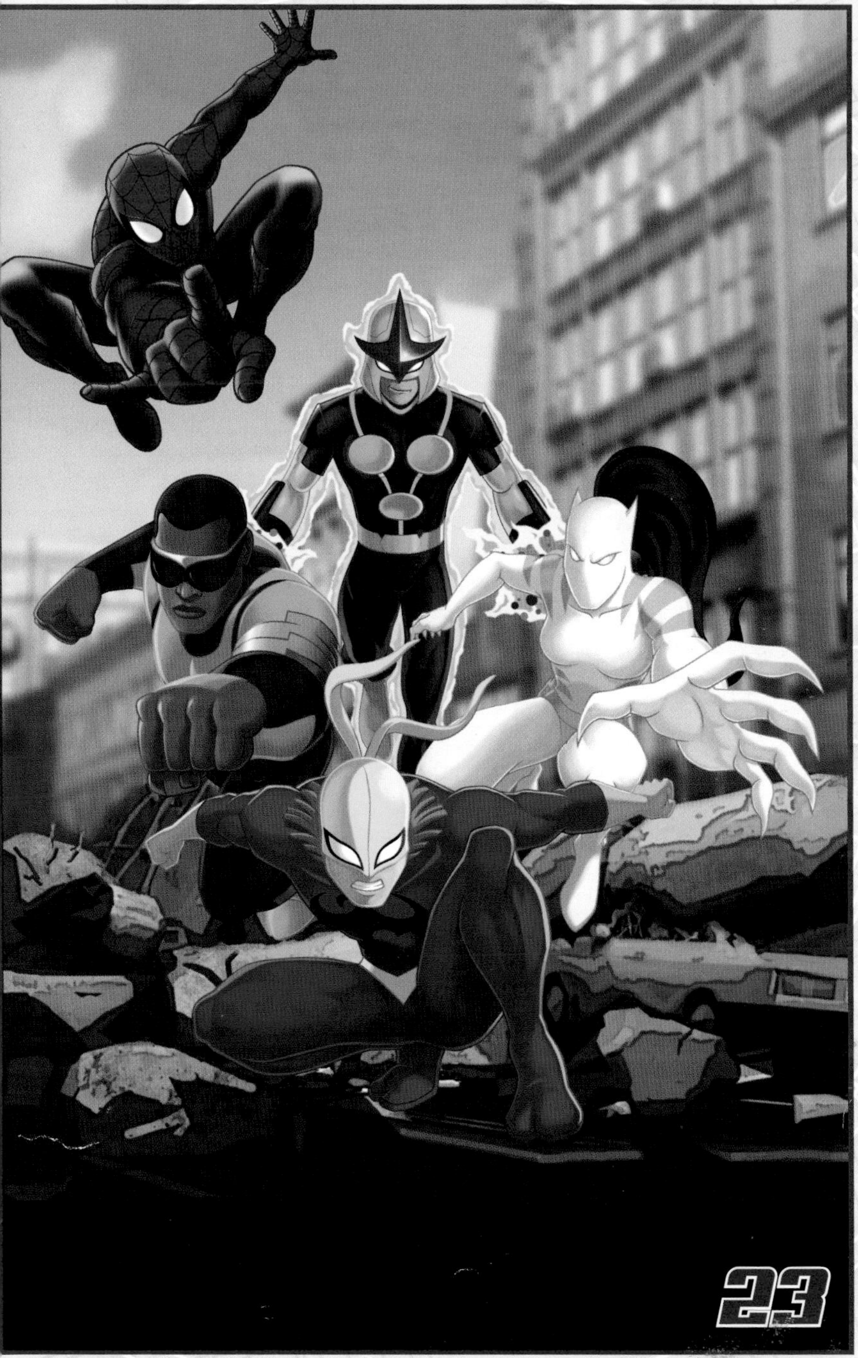
23

Based on "Damage"

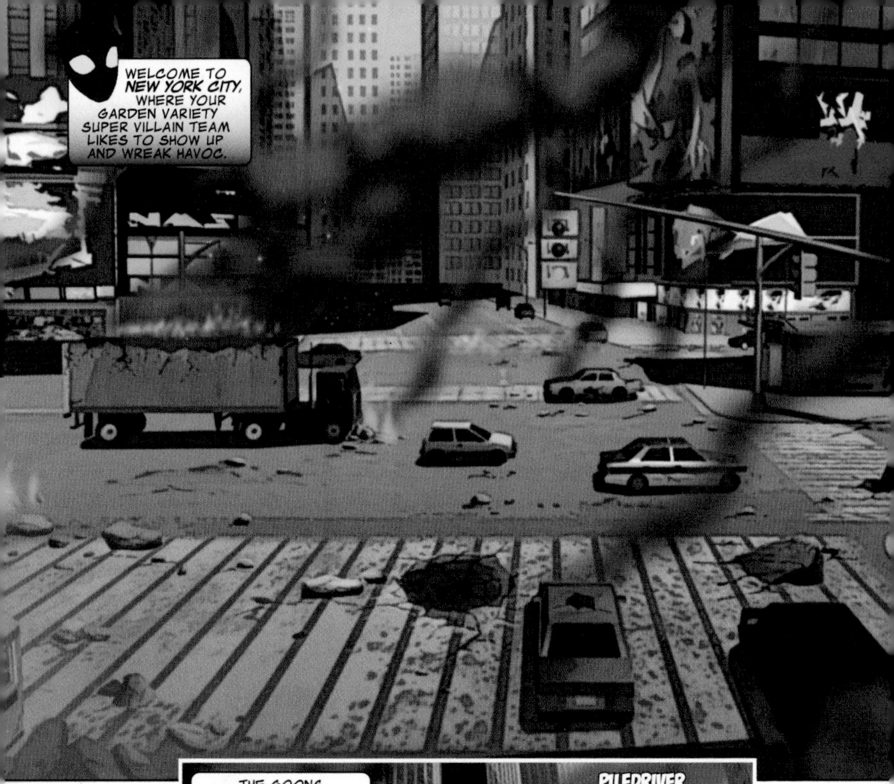
WELCOME TO NEW YORK CITY, WHERE YOUR GARDEN VARIETY SUPER VILLAIN TEAM LIKES TO SHOW UP AND WREAK HAVOC.

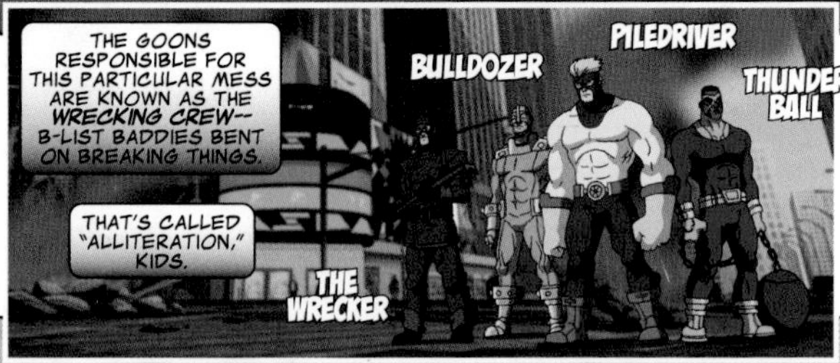
THE GOONS RESPONSIBLE FOR THIS PARTICULAR MESS ARE KNOWN AS THE WRECKING CREW-- B-LIST BADDIES BENT ON BREAKING THINGS.
BULLDOZER
PILEDRIVER
THUNDER BALL
THAT'S CALLED "ALLITERATION," KIDS.
THE WRECKER

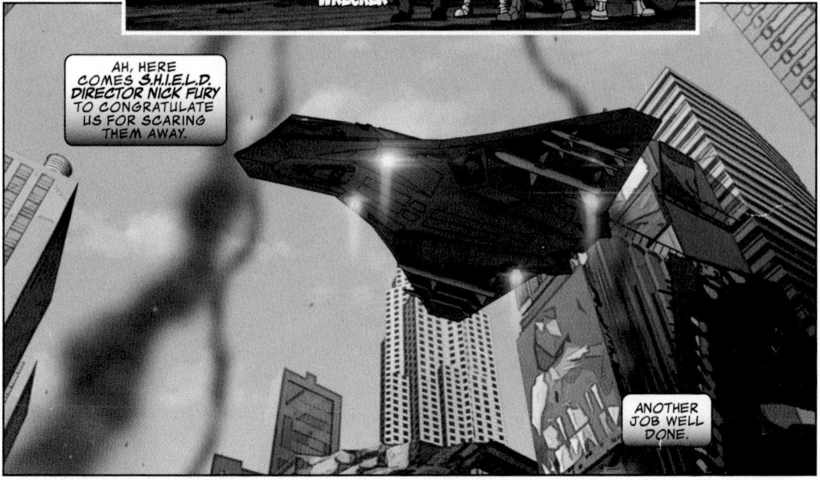
AH, HERE COMES S.H.I.E.L.D. DIRECTOR NICK FURY TO CONGRATULATE US FOR SCARING THEM AWAY.
ANOTHER JOB WELL DONE.

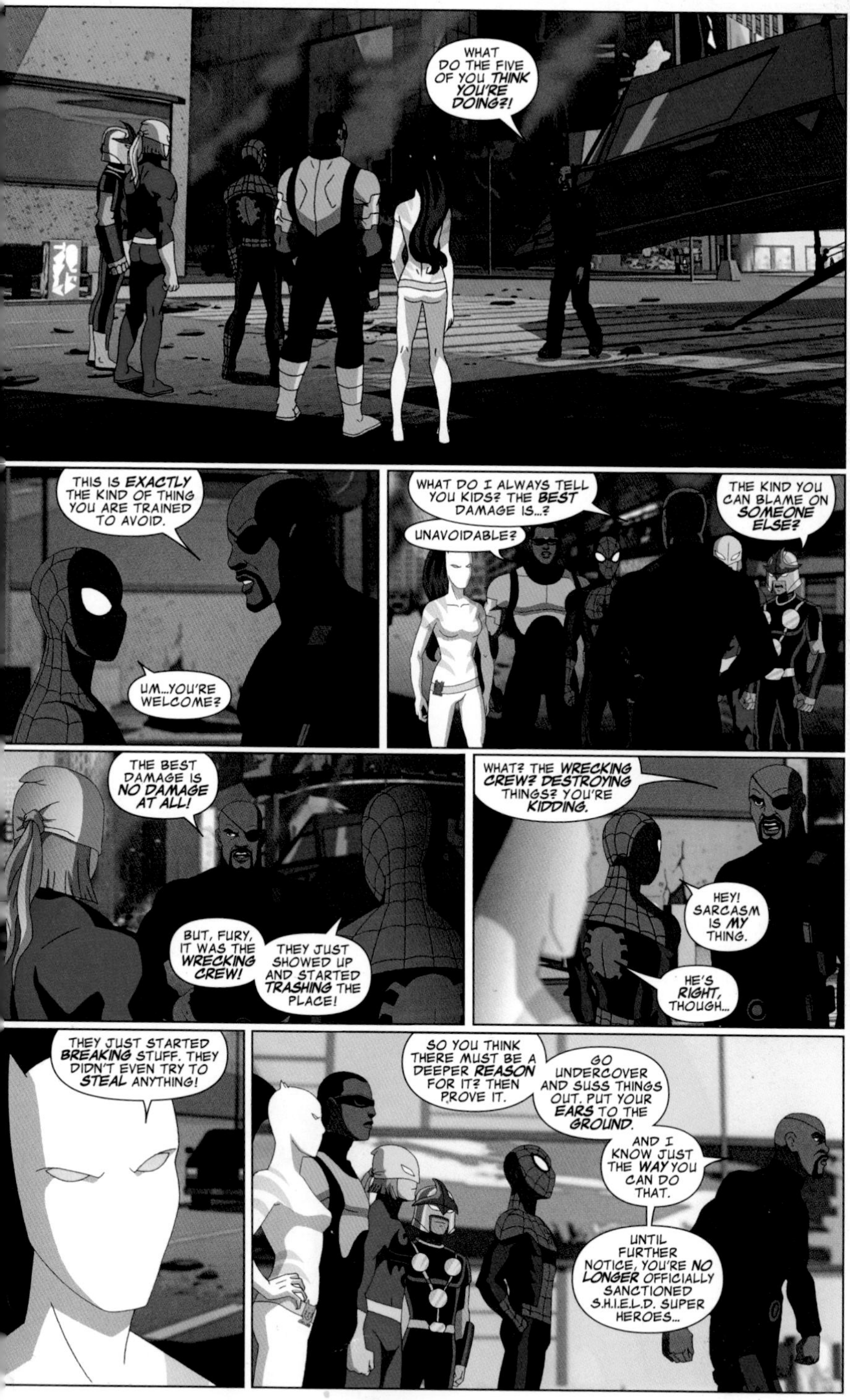

WHAT DO THE FIVE OF YOU THINK YOU'RE DOING?!
THIS IS EXACTLY THE KIND OF THING YOU ARE TRAINED TO AVOID.
UM...YOU'RE WELCOME?
WHAT DO I ALWAYS TELL YOU KIDS? THE BEST DAMAGE IS...?
UNAVOIDABLE?
THE KIND YOU CAN BLAME ON SOMEONE ELSE?
THE BEST DAMAGE IS NO DAMAGE AT ALL!
BUT, FURY, IT WAS THE WRECKING CREW!
THEY JUST SHOWED UP AND STARTED TRASHING THE PLACE!
WHAT? THE WRECKING CREW? DESTROYING THINGS? YOU'RE KIDDING.
HEY! SARCASM IS MY THING.
HE'S RIGHT, THOUGH...
THEY JUST STARTED BREAKING STUFF. THEY DIDN'T EVEN TRY TO STEAL ANYTHING!
SO YOU THINK THERE MUST BE A DEEPER REASON FOR IT? THEN PROVE IT.
GO UNDERCOVER AND SUSS THINGS OUT. PUT YOUR EARS TO THE GROUND.
AND I KNOW JUST THE WAY YOU CAN DO THAT.
UNTIL FURTHER NOTICE, YOU'RE NO LONGER OFFICIALLY SANCTIONED S.H.I.E.L.D. SUPER HEROES...

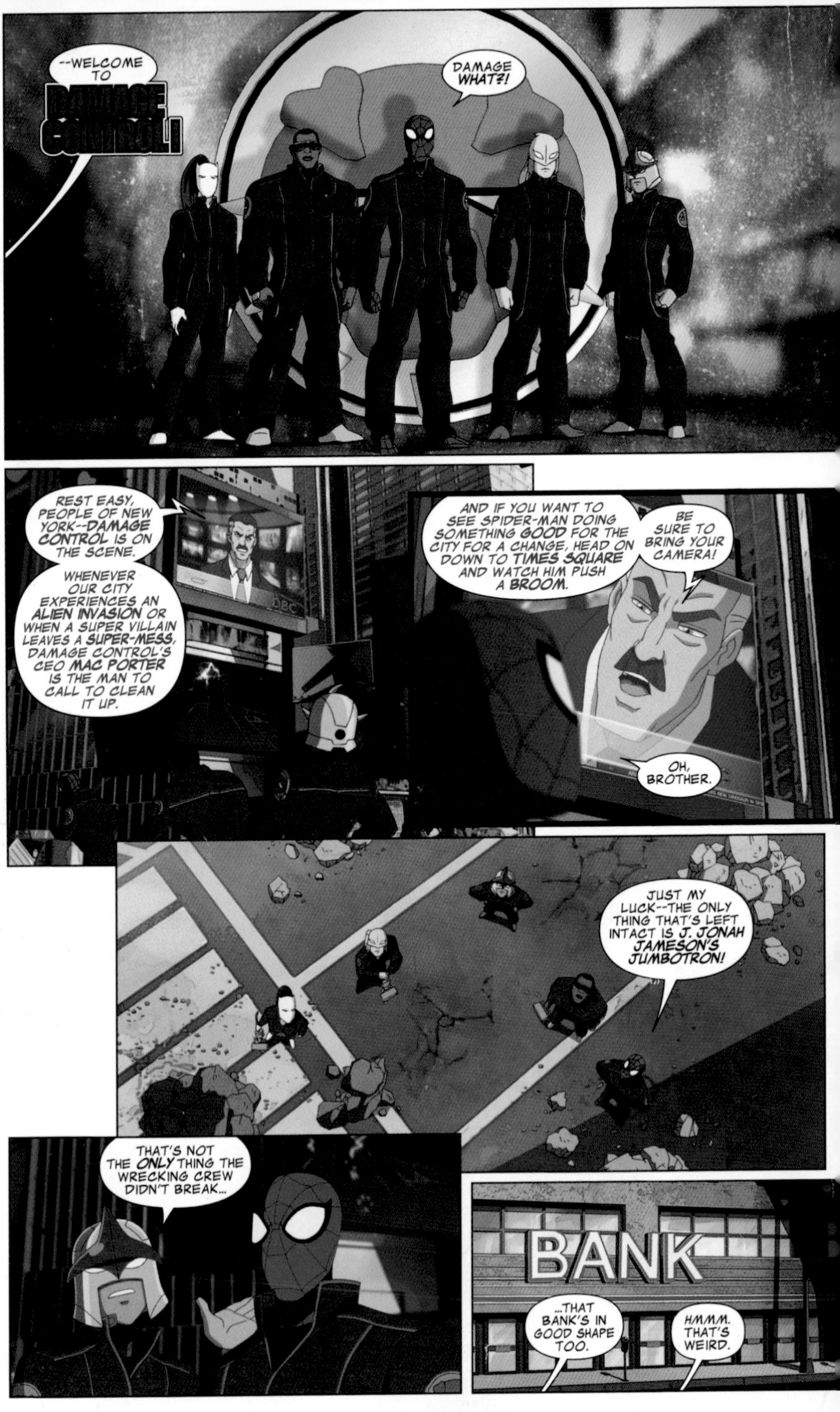
--WELCOME TO DAMAGE CONTROL!
DAMAGE WHAT?!
REST EASY, PEOPLE OF NEW YORK--DAMAGE CONTROL IS ON THE SCENE.
WHENEVER OUR CITY EXPERIENCES AN ALIEN INVASION OR WHEN A SUPER VILLAIN LEAVES A SUPER-MESS, DAMAGE CONTROL'S CEO MAC PORTER IS THE MAN TO CALL TO CLEAN IT UP.
AND IF YOU WANT TO SEE SPIDER-MAN DOING SOMETHING GOOD FOR THE CITY FOR A CHANGE, HEAD ON DOWN TO TIMES SQUARE AND WATCH HIM PUSH A BROOM.
BE SURE TO BRING YOUR CAMERA!
OH, BROTHER.
JUST MY LUCK--THE ONLY THING THAT'S LEFT INTACT IS J. JONAH JAMESON'S JUMBOTRON!
THAT'S NOT THE ONLY THING THE WRECKING CREW DIDN'T BREAK...
BANK
...THAT BANK'S IN GOOD SHAPE TOO.
HMMM. THAT'S WEIRD.

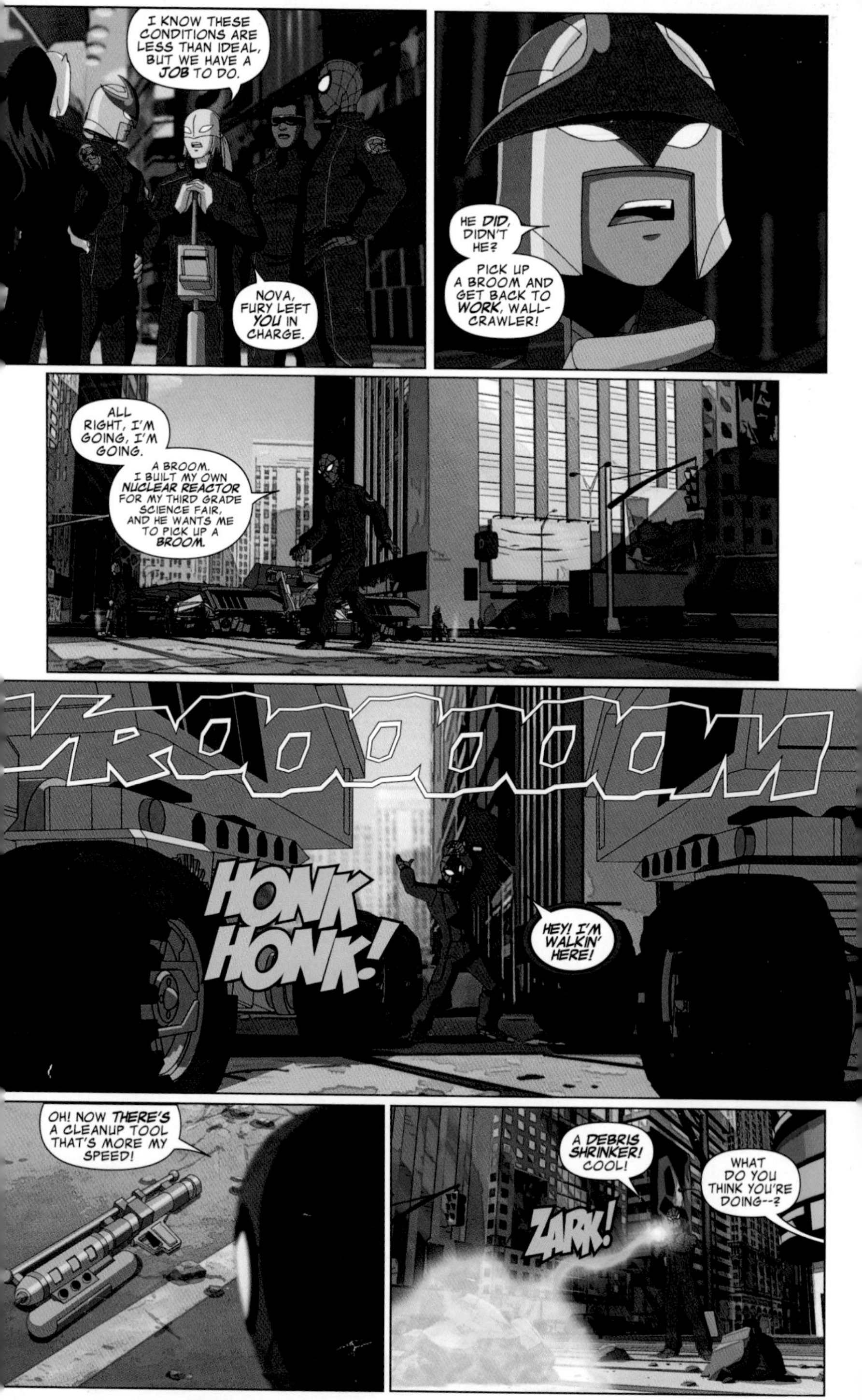
I KNOW THESE CONDITIONS ARE LESS THAN IDEAL, BUT WE HAVE A JOB TO DO.
NOVA, FURY LEFT YOU IN CHARGE.
HE DID, DIDN'T HE?
PICK UP A BROOM AND GET BACK TO WORK, WALL-CRAWLER!
ALL RIGHT, I'M GOING, I'M GOING.
A BROOM. I BUILT MY OWN NUCLEAR REACTOR FOR MY THIRD GRADE SCIENCE FAIR, AND HE WANTS ME TO PICK UP A BROOM.
VROOOOOOOM
HONK HONK!
HEY! I'M WALKIN' HERE!
OH! NOW THERE'S A CLEANUP TOOL THAT'S MORE MY SPEED!
A DEBRIS SHRINKER! COOL!
ZARK!
WHAT DO YOU THINK YOU'RE DOING--?

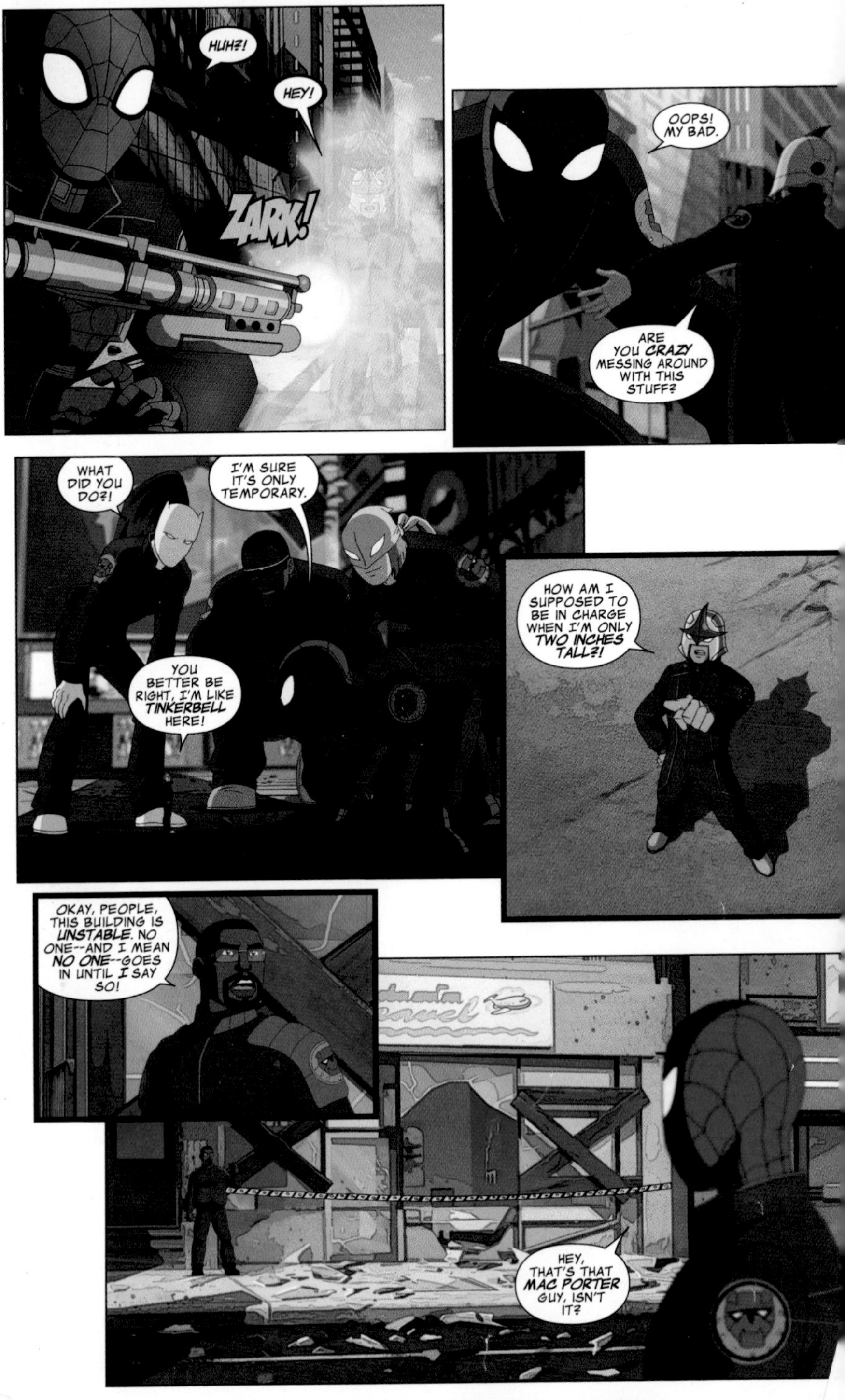
HUH?!
HEY!
ZARK!
OOPS! MY BAD.
ARE YOU CRAZY MESSING AROUND WITH THIS STUFF?
WHAT DID YOU DO?!
I'M SURE IT'S ONLY TEMPORARY.
YOU BETTER BE RIGHT, I'M LIKE TINKERBELL HERE!
HOW AM I SUPPOSED TO BE IN CHARGE WHEN I'M ONLY TWO INCHES TALL?!
OKAY, PEOPLE, THIS BUILDING IS UNSTABLE. NO ONE--AND I MEAN NO ONE--GOES IN UNTIL I SAY SO!
HEY, THAT'S THAT MAC PORTER GUY, ISN'T IT?

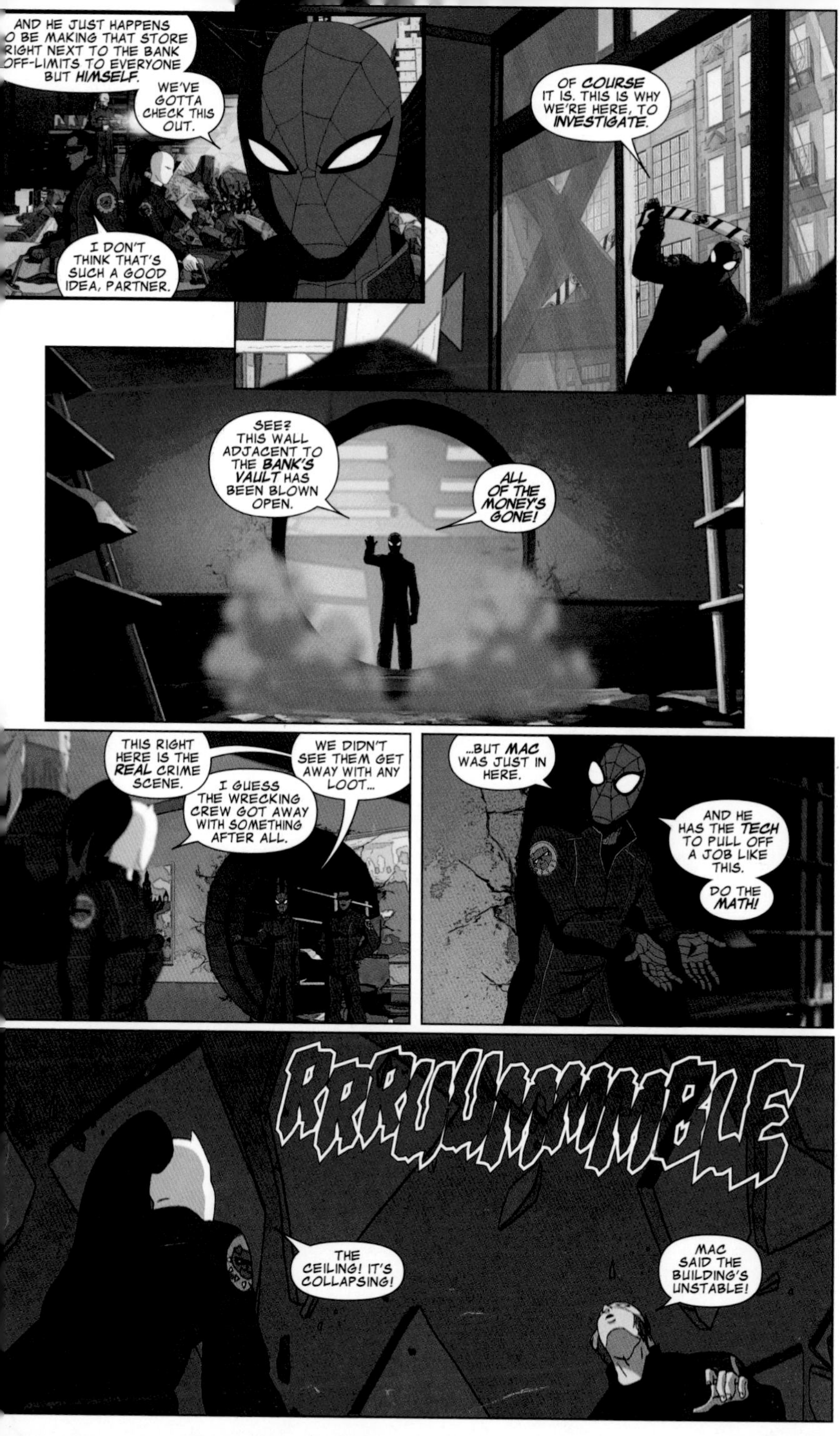

AND HE JUST HAPPENS TO BE MAKING THAT STORE RIGHT NEXT TO THE BANK OFF-LIMITS TO EVERYONE BUT HIMSELF.
WE'VE GOTTA CHECK THIS OUT.
I DON'T THINK THAT'S SUCH A GOOD IDEA, PARTNER.
OF COURSE IT IS. THIS IS WHY WE'RE HERE, TO INVESTIGATE.
SEE? THIS WALL ADJACENT TO THE BANK'S VAULT HAS BEEN BLOWN OPEN.
ALL OF THE MONEY'S GONE!
THIS RIGHT HERE IS THE REAL CRIME SCENE.
WE DIDN'T SEE THEM GET AWAY WITH ANY LOOT...
I GUESS THE WRECKING CREW GOT AWAY WITH SOMETHING AFTER ALL.
...BUT MAC WAS JUST IN HERE.
AND HE HAS THE TECH TO PULL OFF A JOB LIKE THIS.
DO THE MATH!
RRRUMMMBLE
THE CEILING! IT'S COLLAPSING!
MAC SAID THE BUILDING'S UNSTABLE!

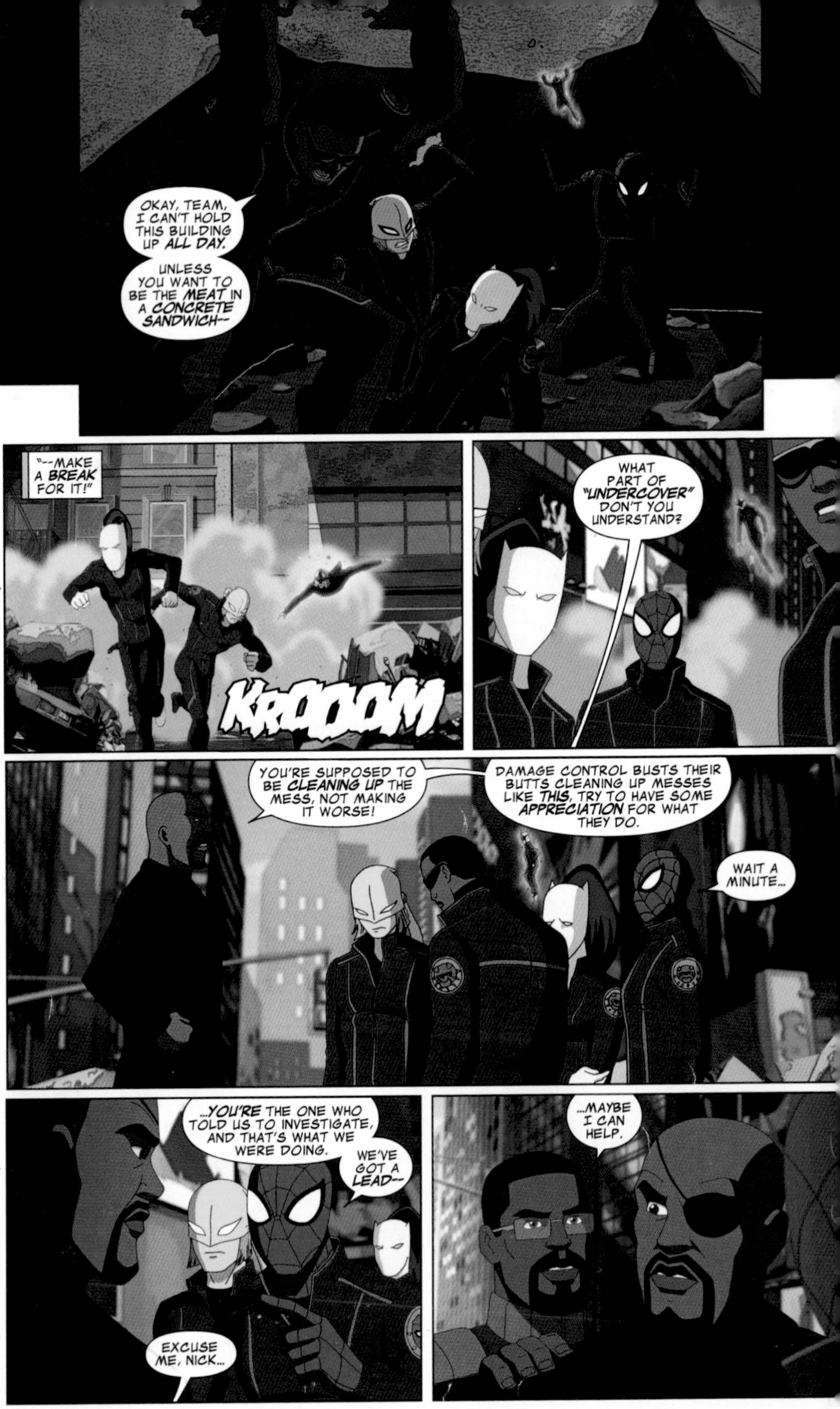
OKAY, TEAM, I CAN'T HOLD THIS BUILDING UP ALL DAY.
UNLESS YOU WANT TO BE THE MEAT IN A CONCRETE SANDWICH--
"--MAKE A BREAK FOR IT!"
KROOOM
WHAT PART OF "UNDERCOVER" DON'T YOU UNDERSTAND?
YOU'RE SUPPOSED TO BE CLEANING UP THE MESS, NOT MAKING IT WORSE!
DAMAGE CONTROL BUSTS THEIR BUTTS CLEANING UP MESSES LIKE THIS, TRY TO HAVE SOME APPRECIATION FOR WHAT THEY DO.
WAIT A MINUTE...
...YOU'RE THE ONE WHO TOLD US TO INVESTIGATE, AND THAT'S WHAT WE WERE DOING.
WE'VE GOT A LEAD--
EXCUSE ME, NICK...
...MAYBE I CAN HELP.

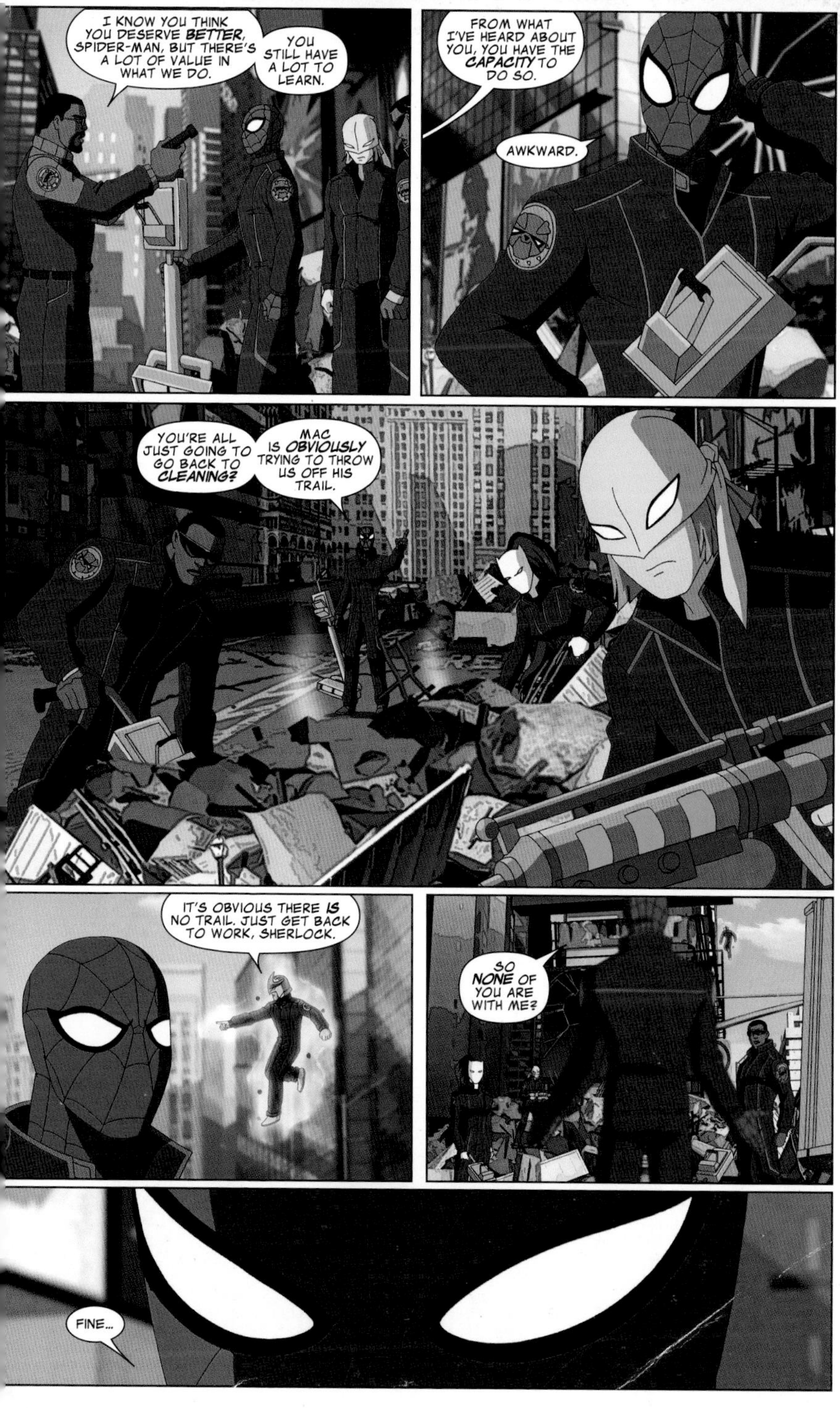
I KNOW YOU THINK YOU DESERVE BETTER, SPIDER-MAN, BUT THERE'S A LOT OF VALUE IN WHAT WE DO.
YOU STILL HAVE A LOT TO LEARN.
FROM WHAT I'VE HEARD ABOUT YOU, YOU HAVE THE CAPACITY TO DO SO.
AWKWARD.
YOU'RE ALL JUST GOING TO GO BACK TO CLEANING?
MAC IS OBVIOUSLY TRYING TO THROW US OFF HIS TRAIL.
IT'S OBVIOUS THERE IS NO TRAIL. JUST GET BACK TO WORK, SHERLOCK.
SO NONE OF YOU ARE WITH ME?
FINE...

"...I'LL SOLVE THIS MYSTERY ON MY OWN."
DAMAGE CONTROL HQ.
LOOKS LIKE MY TEAM WON'T BE CONVINCED UNTIL I ACTUALLY FIND THE MONEY.
THIS IS AS GOOD A PLACE TO LOOK AS ANY.
MAC
I ADMIT, HE'S RATHER CONSPICUOUS FOR A SECRET SUPER VILLAIN.
GOOD. IT'LL BE A QUICK IN-AND-OUT. NO ONE WILL EVER KNOW I WAS HERE.
INTRUDER ALERT! INTRUDER ALERT!
SO MUCH FOR THAT.
FWOOSH
FWOOSH
FWOOSH
YAAAAAA!
BRA-KOOM!

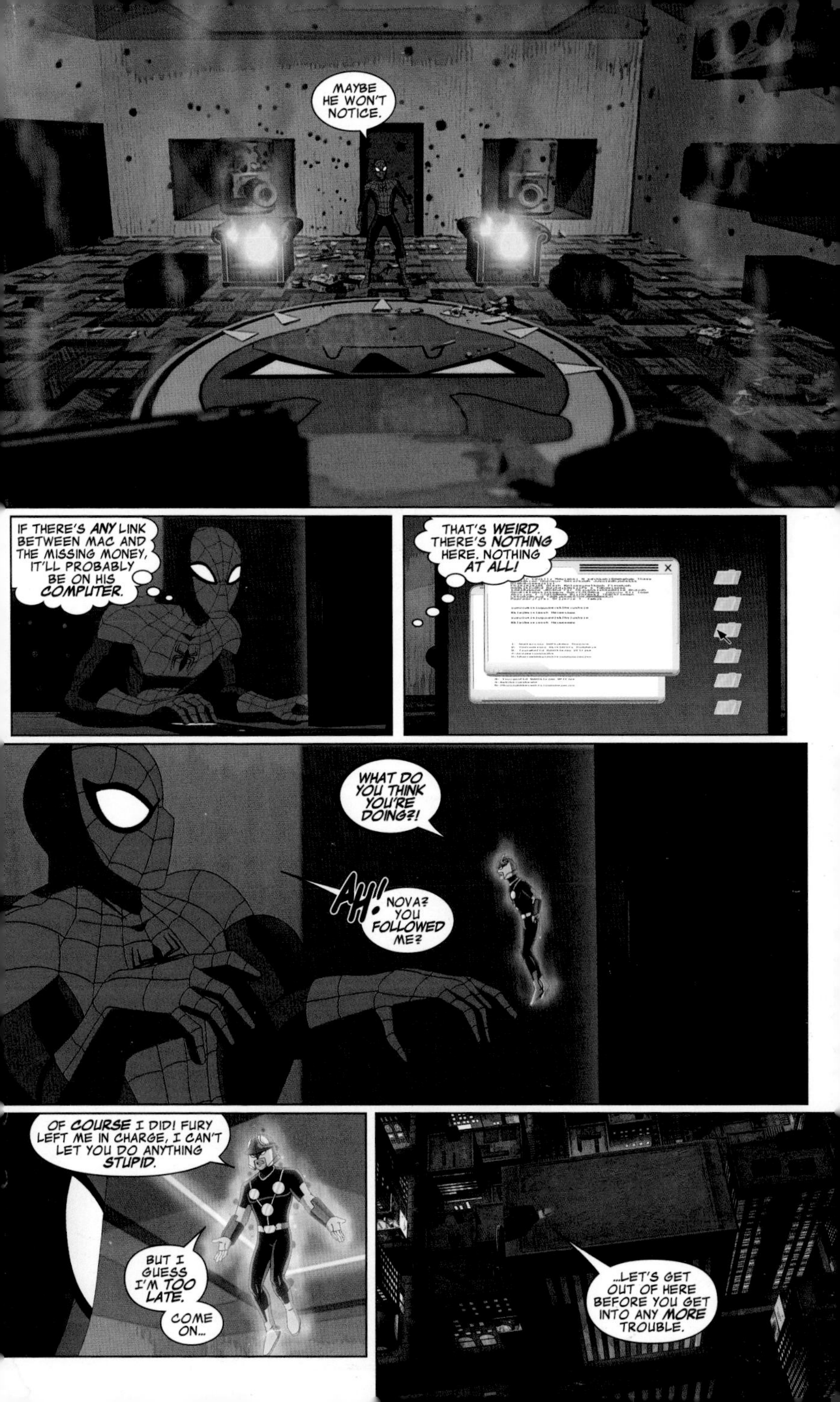

MAYBE HE WON'T NOTICE.
IF THERE'S ANY LINK BETWEEN MAC AND THE MISSING MONEY, IT'LL PROBABLY BE ON HIS COMPUTER.
THAT'S WEIRD. THERE'S NOTHING HERE. NOTHING AT ALL!
WHAT DO YOU THINK YOU'RE DOING?!
AH!
NOVA? YOU FOLLOWED ME?
OF COURSE I DID! FURY LEFT ME IN CHARGE, I CAN'T LET YOU DO ANYTHING STUPID.
BUT I GUESS I'M TOO LATE.
COME ON...
...LET'S GET OUT OF HERE BEFORE YOU GET INTO ANY MORE TROUBLE.

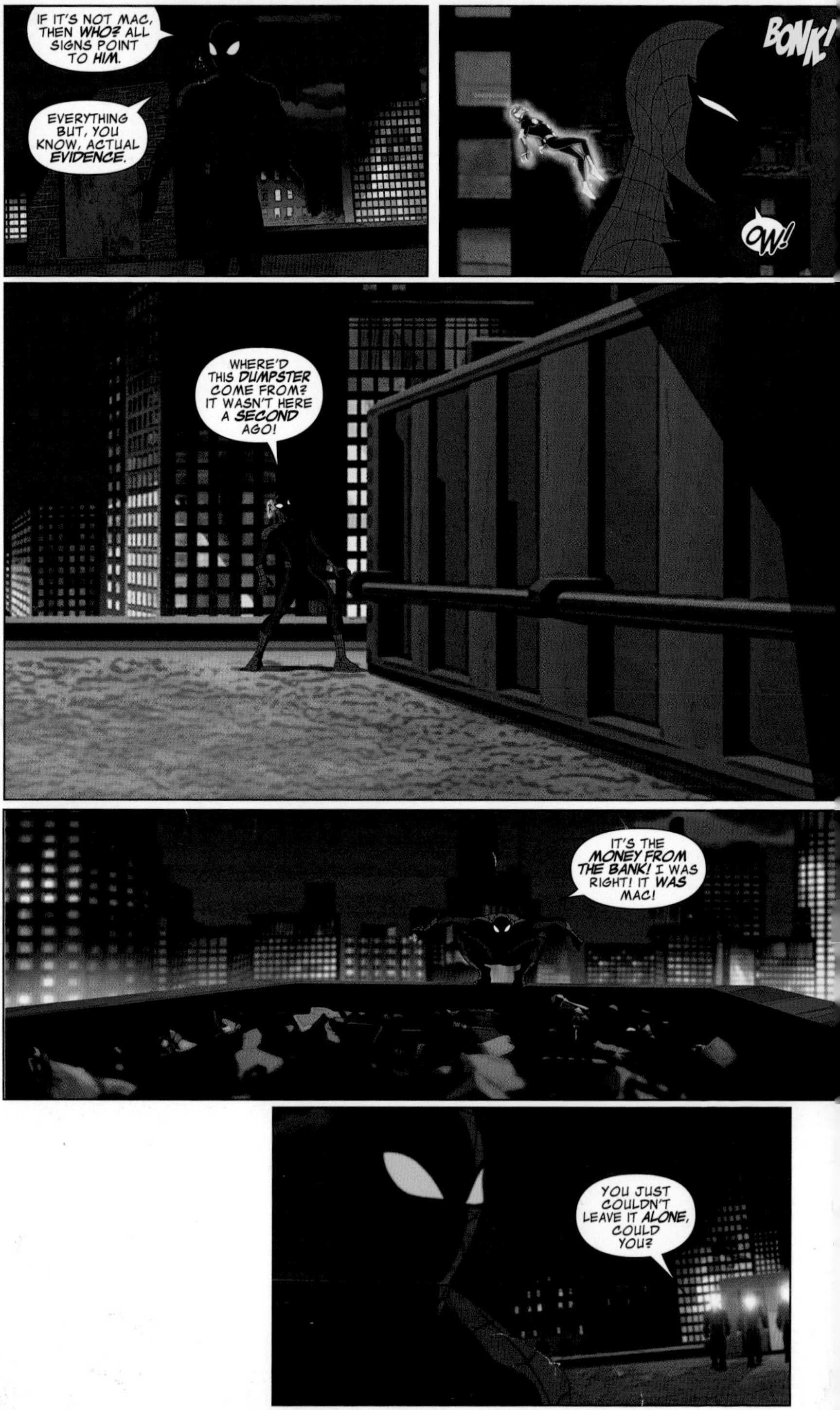
IF IT'S NOT MAC, THEN WHO? ALL SIGNS POINT TO HIM.
EVERYTHING BUT, YOU KNOW, ACTUAL EVIDENCE.
BONK!
OW!
WHERE'D THIS DUMPSTER COME FROM? IT WASN'T HERE A SECOND AGO!
IT'S THE MONEY FROM THE BANK! I WAS RIGHT! IT WAS MAC!
YOU JUST COULDN'T LEAVE IT ALONE, COULD YOU?

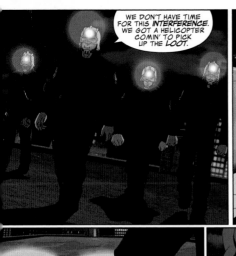

WE DON'T HAVE TIME FOR THIS *INTERFERENCE*. WE GOT A HELICOPTER COMIN' TO PICK UP THE *LOOT*.

LOOK, TELL YOUR BOSS THE GIG IS UP.

IF YOU SURRENDER, NO ONE WILL GET HURT.

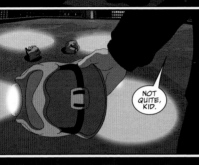

NOT QUITE, KID.

HUH?

THE **WRECKING CREW!**

THAT'S RIGHT. SO MUCH FOR NO ONE GETTING *HURT*, HUH?

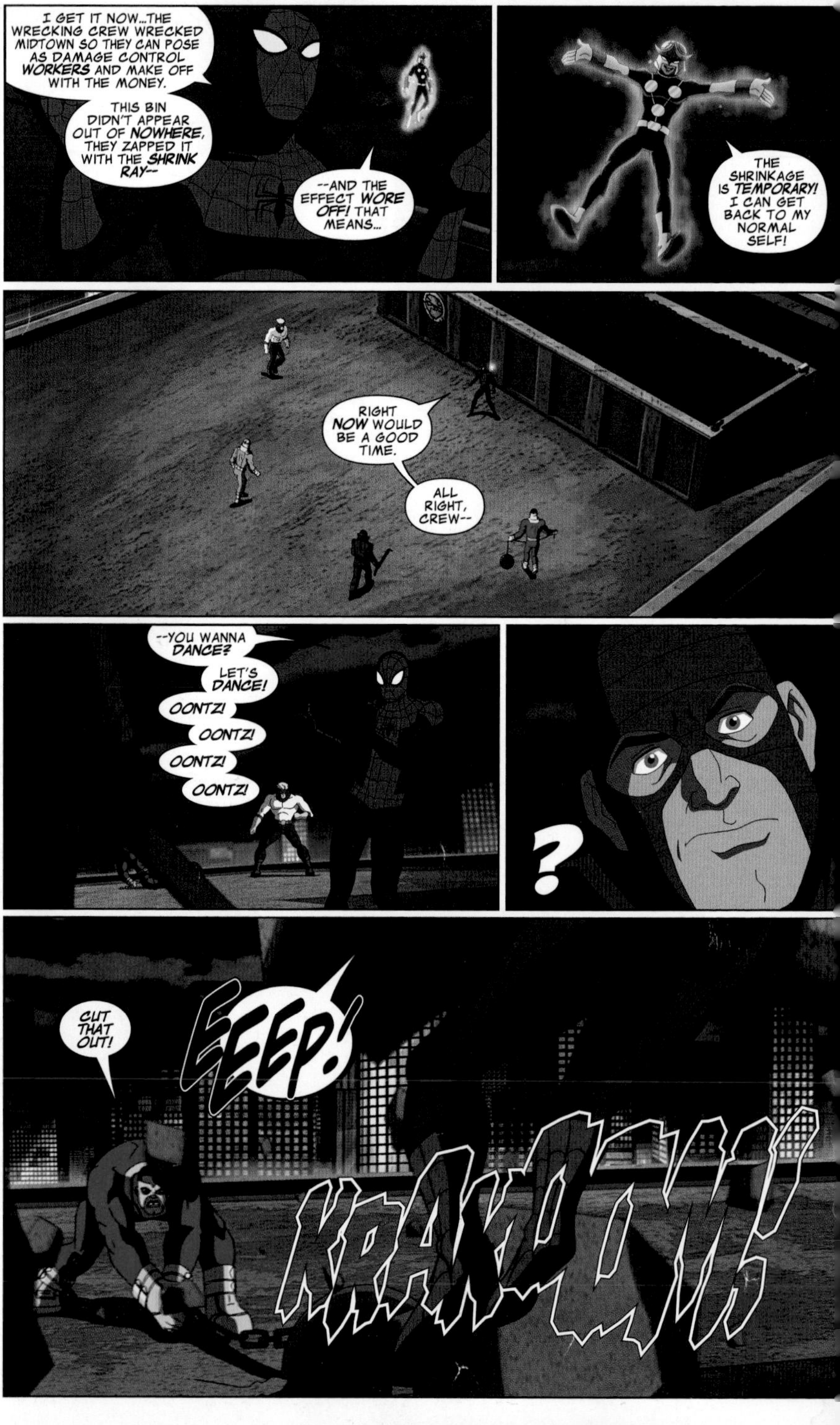
I GET IT NOW...THE WRECKING CREW WRECKED MIDTOWN SO THEY CAN POSE AS DAMAGE CONTROL WORKERS AND MAKE OFF WITH THE MONEY.
THIS BIN DIDN'T APPEAR OUT OF NOWHERE, THEY ZAPPED IT WITH THE SHRINK RAY--
--AND THE EFFECT WORE OFF! THAT MEANS...
THE SHRINKAGE IS TEMPORARY! I CAN GET BACK TO MY NORMAL SELF!
RIGHT NOW WOULD BE A GOOD TIME.
ALL RIGHT, CREW--
--YOU WANNA DANCE?
LET'S DANCE!
OONTZ!
OONTZ!
OONTZ!
OONTZ!
?
CUT THAT OUT!
EEEP!
KRAKOOM!

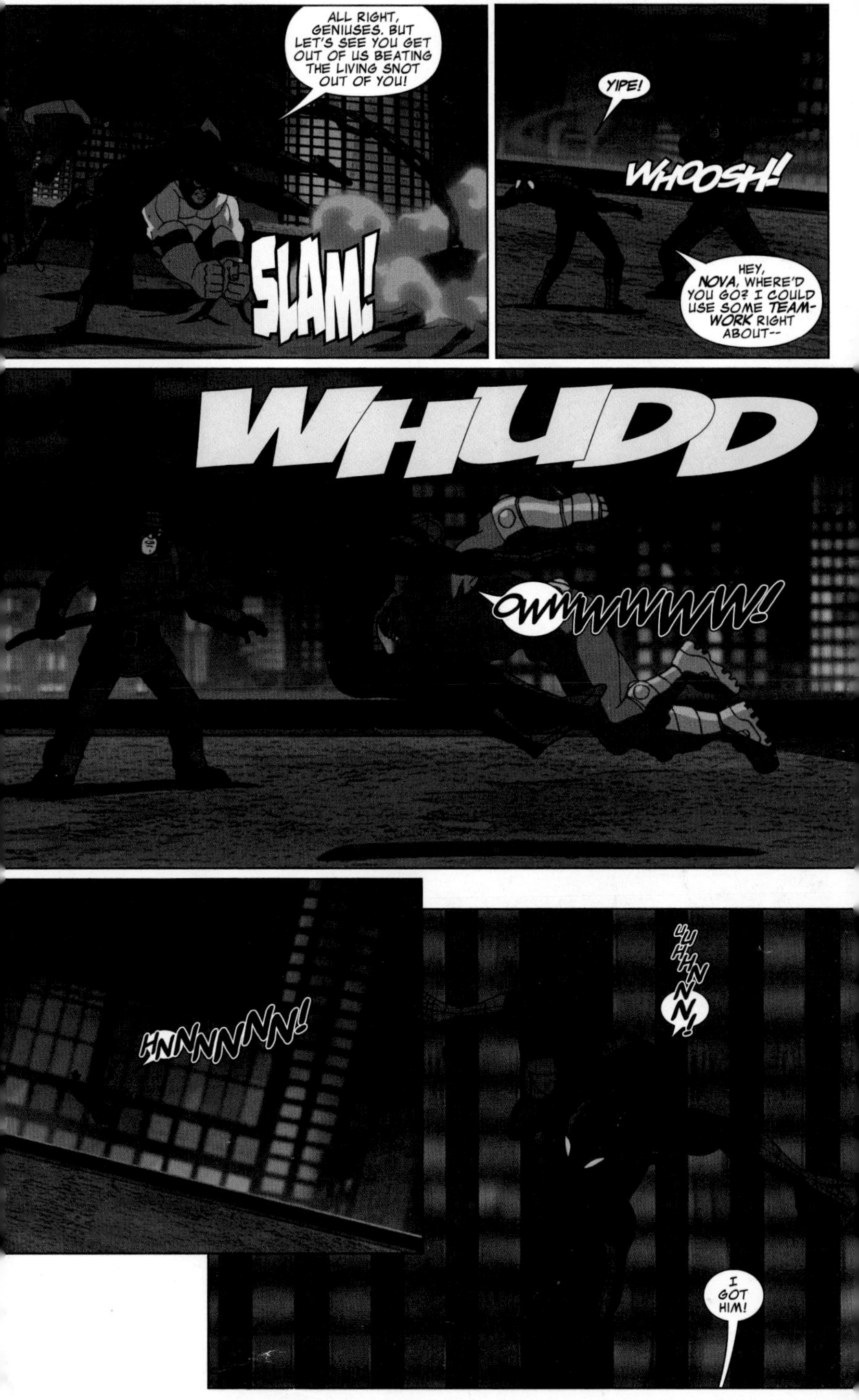
ALL RIGHT, GENIUSES. BUT LET'S SEE YOU GET OUT OF US BEATING THE LIVING SNOT OUT OF YOU!
SLAM!
YIPE!
WHOOSH!
HEY, NOVA, WHERE'D YOU GO? I COULD USE SOME TEAM-WORK RIGHT ABOUT--
WHUDD
OWWWWWWW!
HNNNNNN!
UHHNNN!
I GOT HIM!

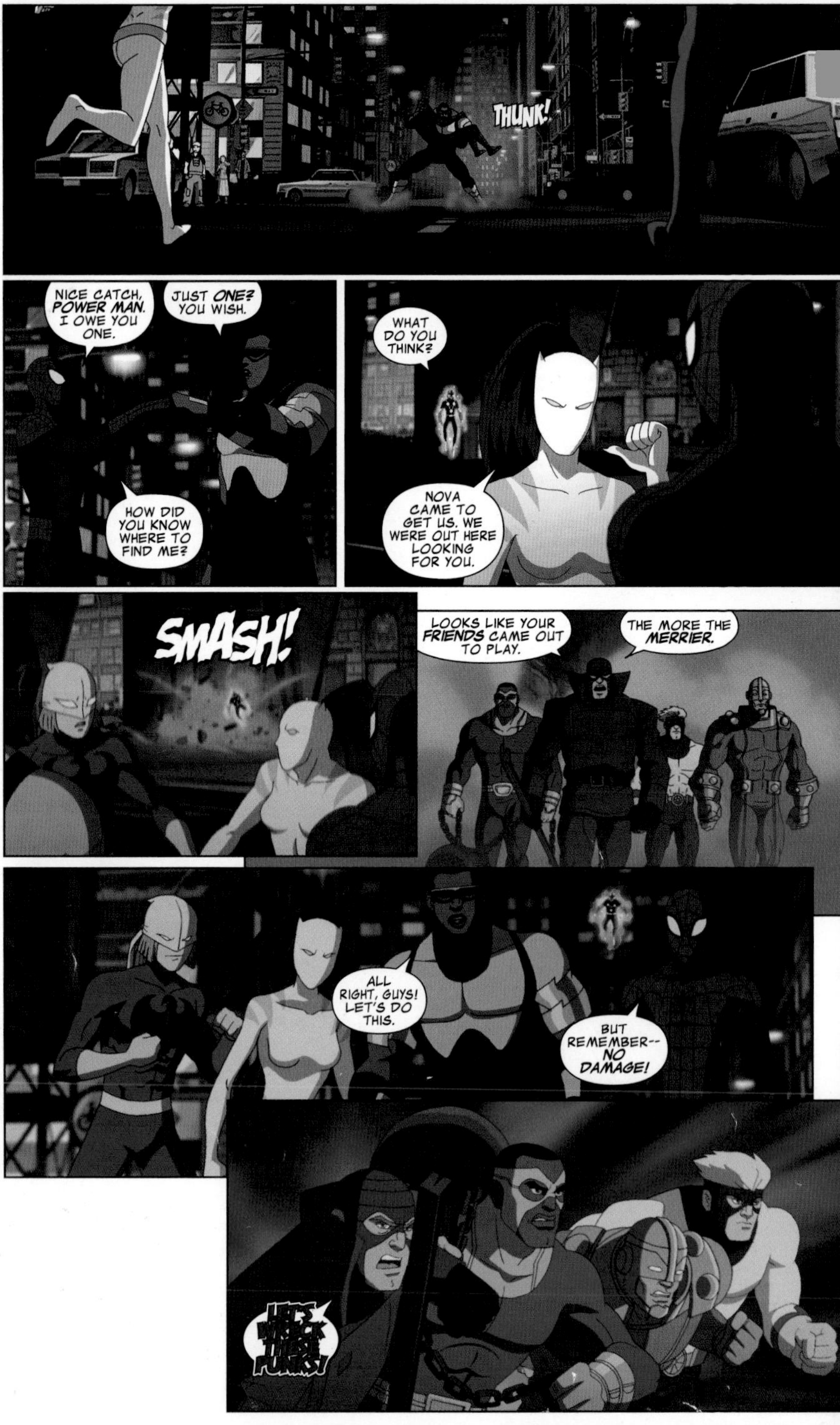
THUNK!
NICE CATCH, POWER MAN. I OWE YOU ONE.
JUST ONE? YOU WISH.
HOW DID YOU KNOW WHERE TO FIND ME?
WHAT DO YOU THINK?
NOVA CAME TO GET US. WE WERE OUT HERE LOOKING FOR YOU.
SMASH!
LOOKS LIKE YOUR FRIENDS CAME OUT TO PLAY.
THE MORE THE MERRIER.
ALL RIGHT, GUYS! LET'S DO THIS.
BUT REMEMBER-- NO DAMAGE!
LET'S WRECK THESE PUNKS!

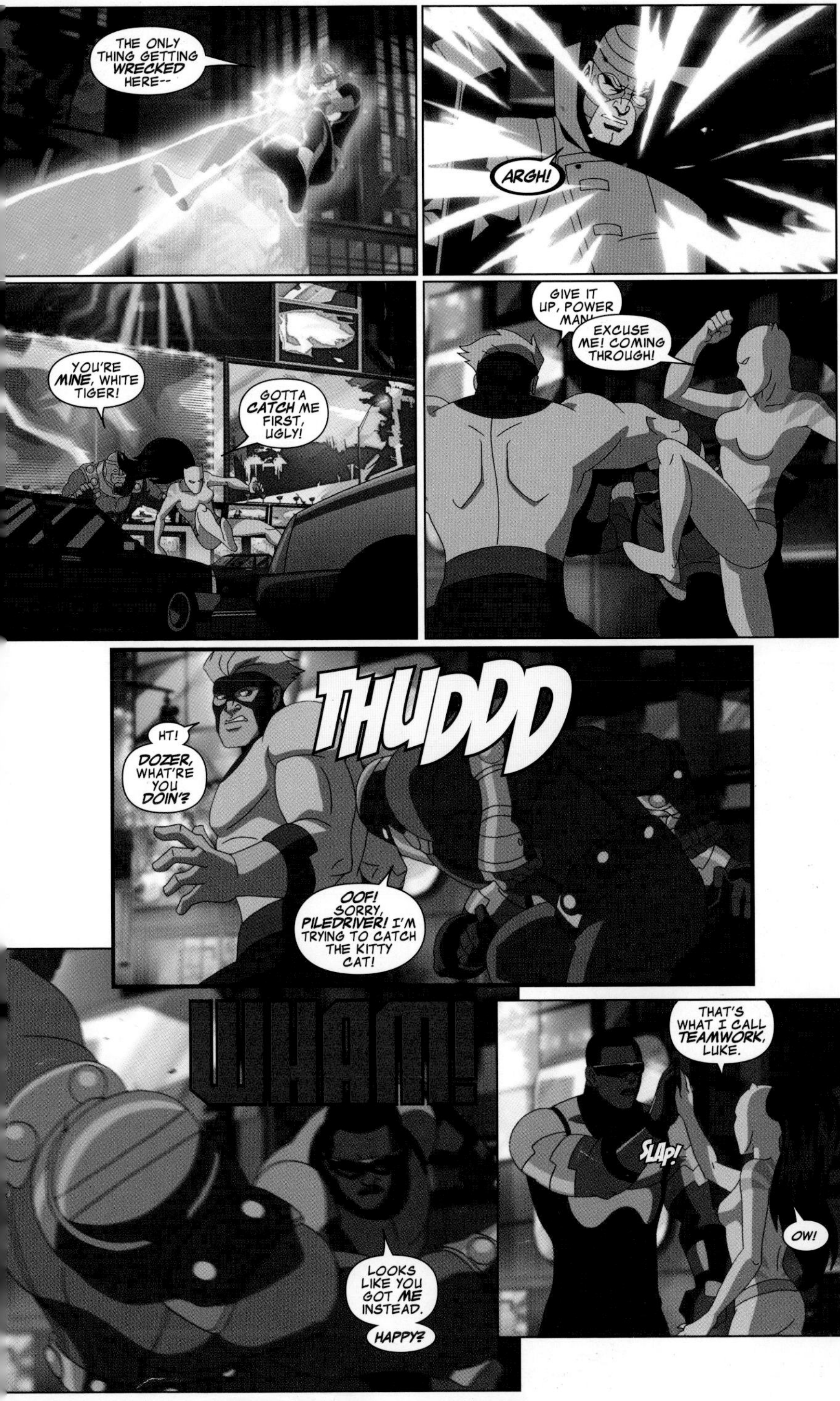
THE ONLY THING GETTING WRECKED HERE--
ARGH!
YOU'RE MINE, WHITE TIGER!
GOTTA CATCH ME FIRST, UGLY!
GIVE IT UP, POWER MAN!
EXCUSE ME! COMING THROUGH!
THUDDD
HT! DOZER, WHAT'RE YOU DOIN'?
OOF! SORRY, PILEDRIVER! I'M TRYING TO CATCH THE KITTY CAT!
WHAM!
LOOKS LIKE YOU GOT ME INSTEAD.
HAPPY?
THAT'S WHAT I CALL TEAMWORK, LUKE.
SLAP!
OW!

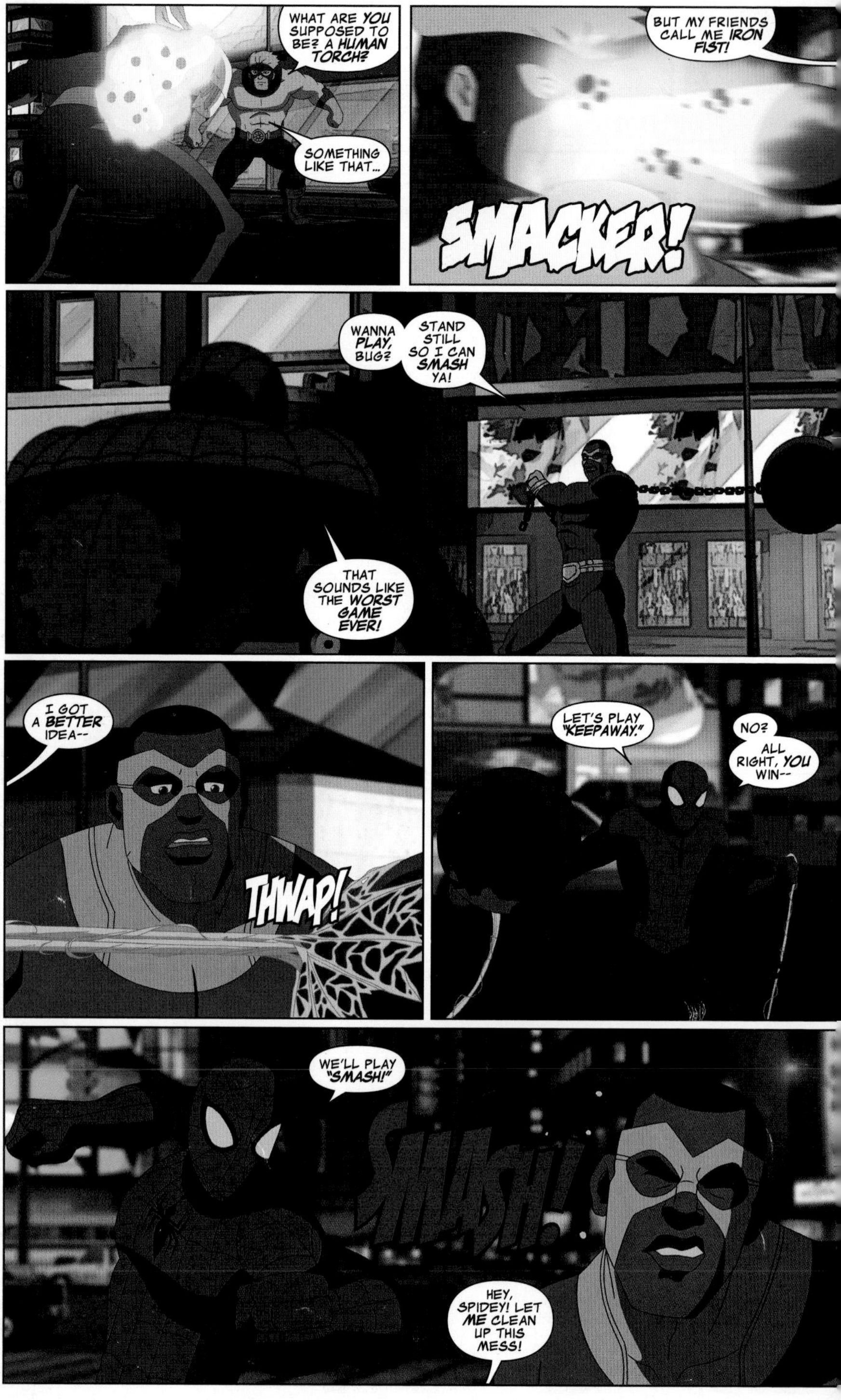
WHAT ARE YOU SUPPOSED TO BE? A HUMAN TORCH?
SOMETHING LIKE THAT...
BUT MY FRIENDS CALL ME IRON FIST!
SMACKER!
WANNA PLAY, BUG?
STAND STILL SO I CAN SMASH YA!
THAT SOUNDS LIKE THE WORST GAME EVER!
I GOT A BETTER IDEA--
THWAP!
LET'S PLAY "KEEPAWAY."
NO? ALL RIGHT, YOU WIN--
WE'LL PLAY "SMASH!"
SMASH!
HEY, SPIDEY! LET ME CLEAN UP THIS MESS!

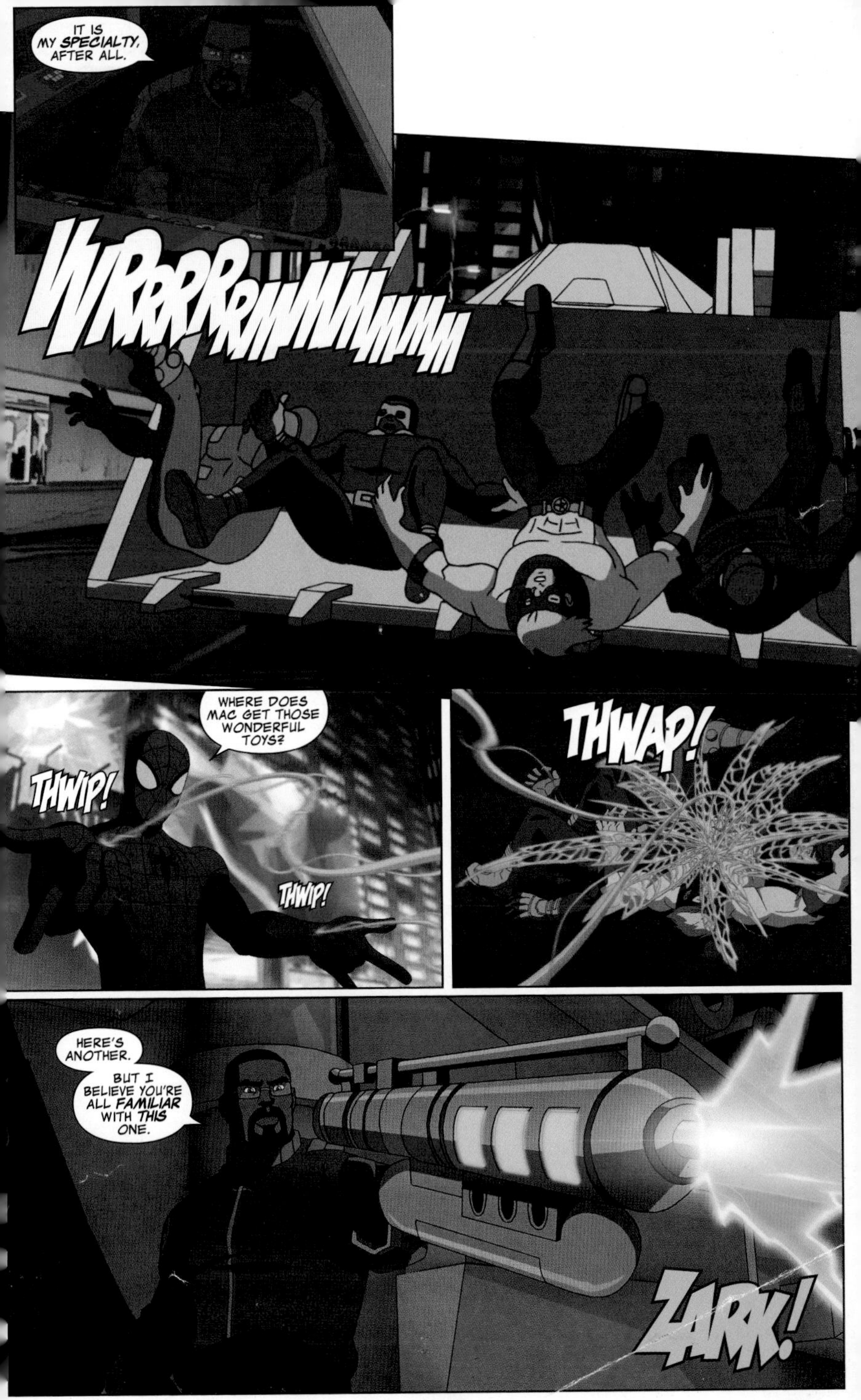

IT IS MY SPECIALTY, AFTER ALL.
VVRRRRRRMMMMMMMMM
WHERE DOES MAC GET THOSE WONDERFUL TOYS?
THWIP!
THWIP!
THWAP!
HERE'S ANOTHER.
BUT I BELIEVE YOU'RE ALL FAMILIAR WITH THIS ONE.
ZARK!

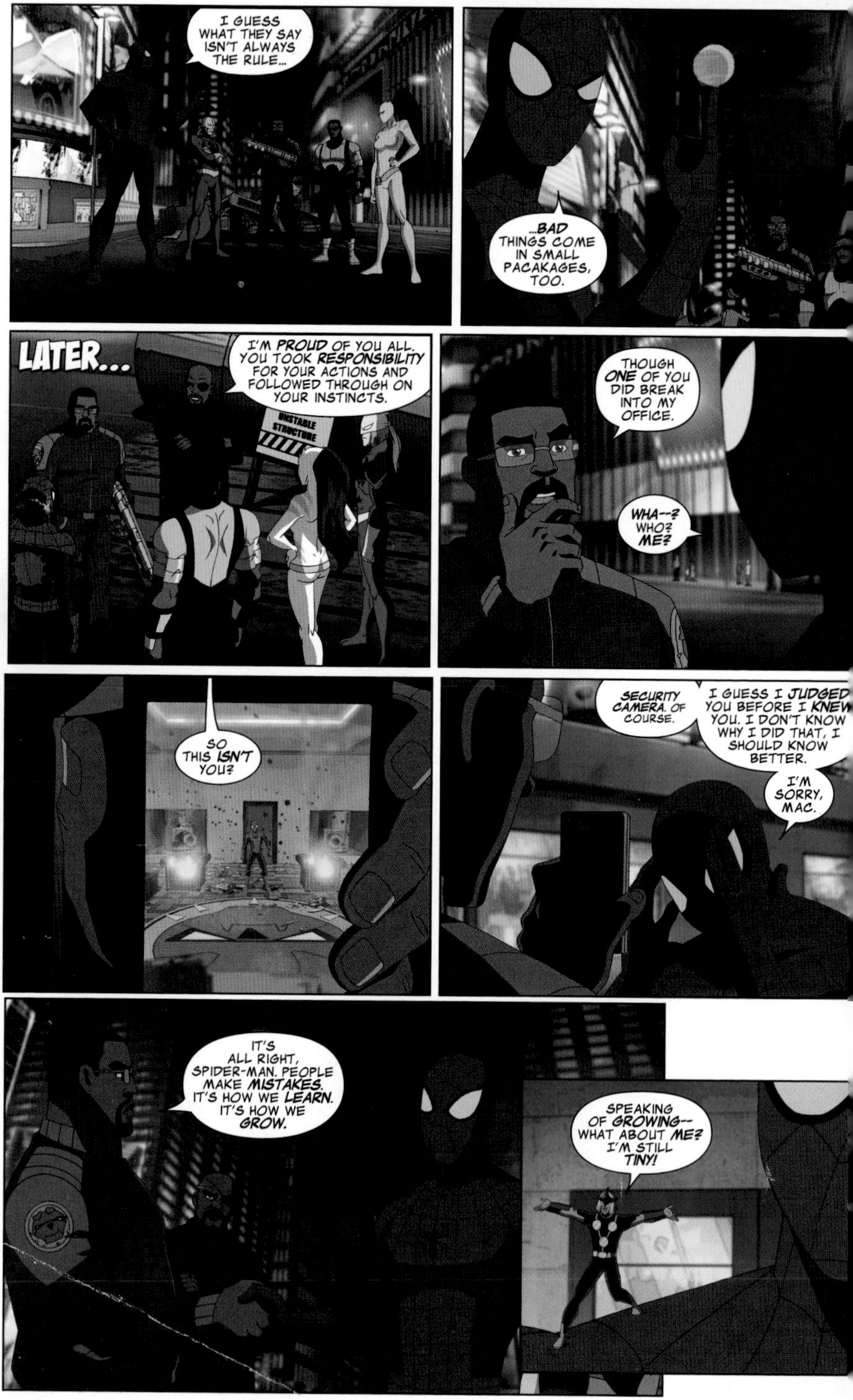
I GUESS WHAT THEY SAY ISN'T ALWAYS THE RULE...
...BAD THINGS COME IN SMALL PACAKAGES, TOO.
LATER...
I'M PROUD OF YOU ALL. YOU TOOK RESPONSIBILITY FOR YOUR ACTIONS AND FOLLOWED THROUGH ON YOUR INSTINCTS.
UNSTABLE STRUCTURE
THOUGH ONE OF YOU DID BREAK INTO MY OFFICE.
WHA--? WHO? ME?
SO THIS ISN'T YOU?
SECURITY CAMERA. OF COURSE.
I GUESS I JUDGED YOU BEFORE I KNEW YOU. I DON'T KNOW WHY I DID THAT, I SHOULD KNOW BETTER.
I'M SORRY, MAC.
IT'S ALL RIGHT, SPIDER-MAN. PEOPLE MAKE MISTAKES. IT'S HOW WE LEARN. IT'S HOW WE GROW.
SPEAKING OF GROWING-- WHAT ABOUT ME? I'M STILL TINY!

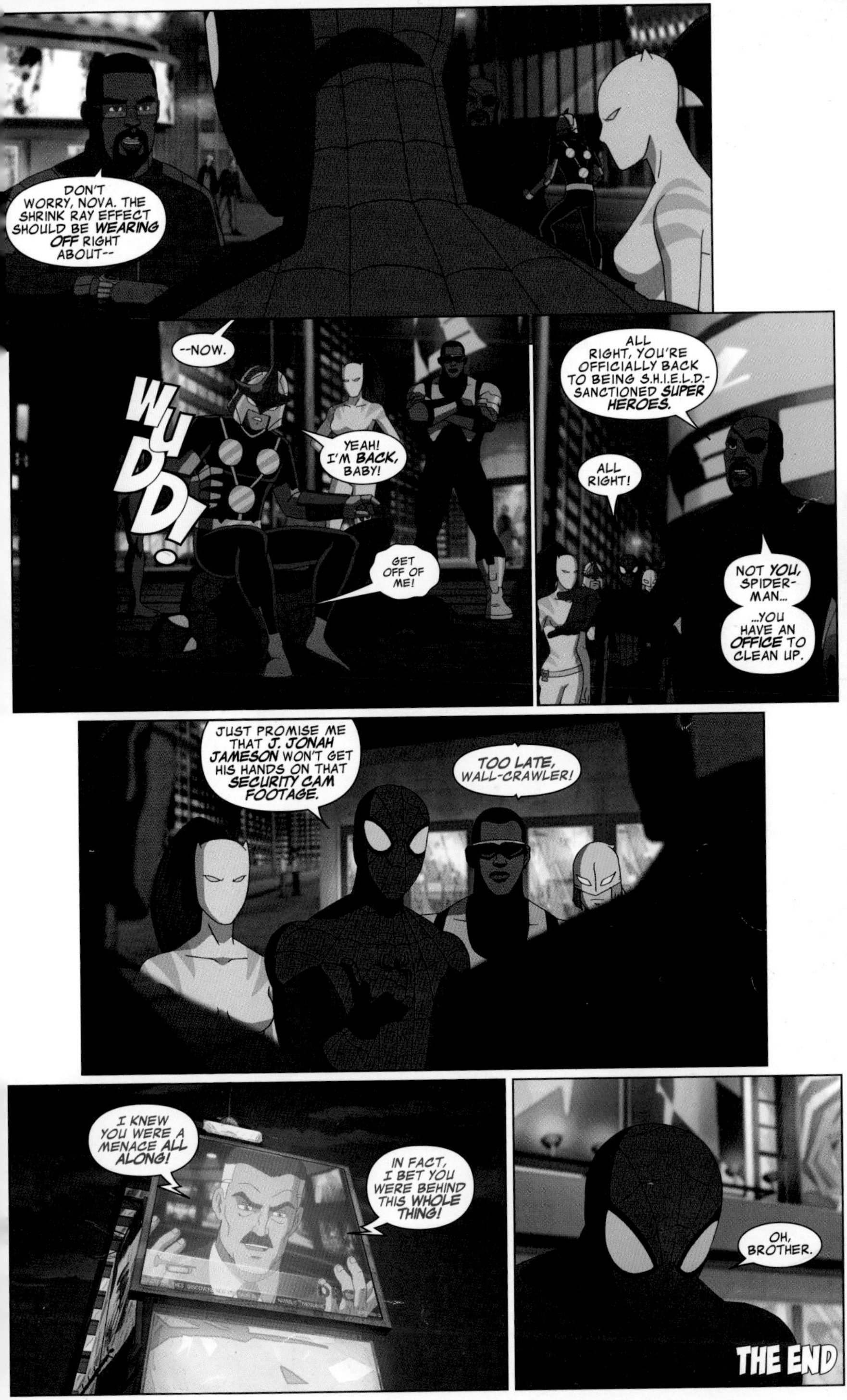
DON'T WORRY, NOVA. THE SHRINK RAY EFFECT SHOULD BE WEARING OFF RIGHT ABOUT--
--NOW.
WUDD!
YEAH! I'M BACK, BABY!
GET OFF OF ME!
ALL RIGHT, YOU'RE OFFICIALLY BACK TO BEING S.H.I.E.L.D.-SANCTIONED SUPER HEROES.
ALL RIGHT!
NOT YOU, SPIDER-MAN...
...YOU HAVE AN OFFICE TO CLEAN UP.
JUST PROMISE ME THAT J. JONAH JAMESON WON'T GET HIS HANDS ON THAT SECURITY CAM FOOTAGE.
TOO LATE, WALL-CRAWLER!
I KNEW YOU WERE A MENACE ALL ALONG!
IN FACT, I BET YOU WERE BEHIND THIS WHOLE THING!
OH, BROTHER.
THE END

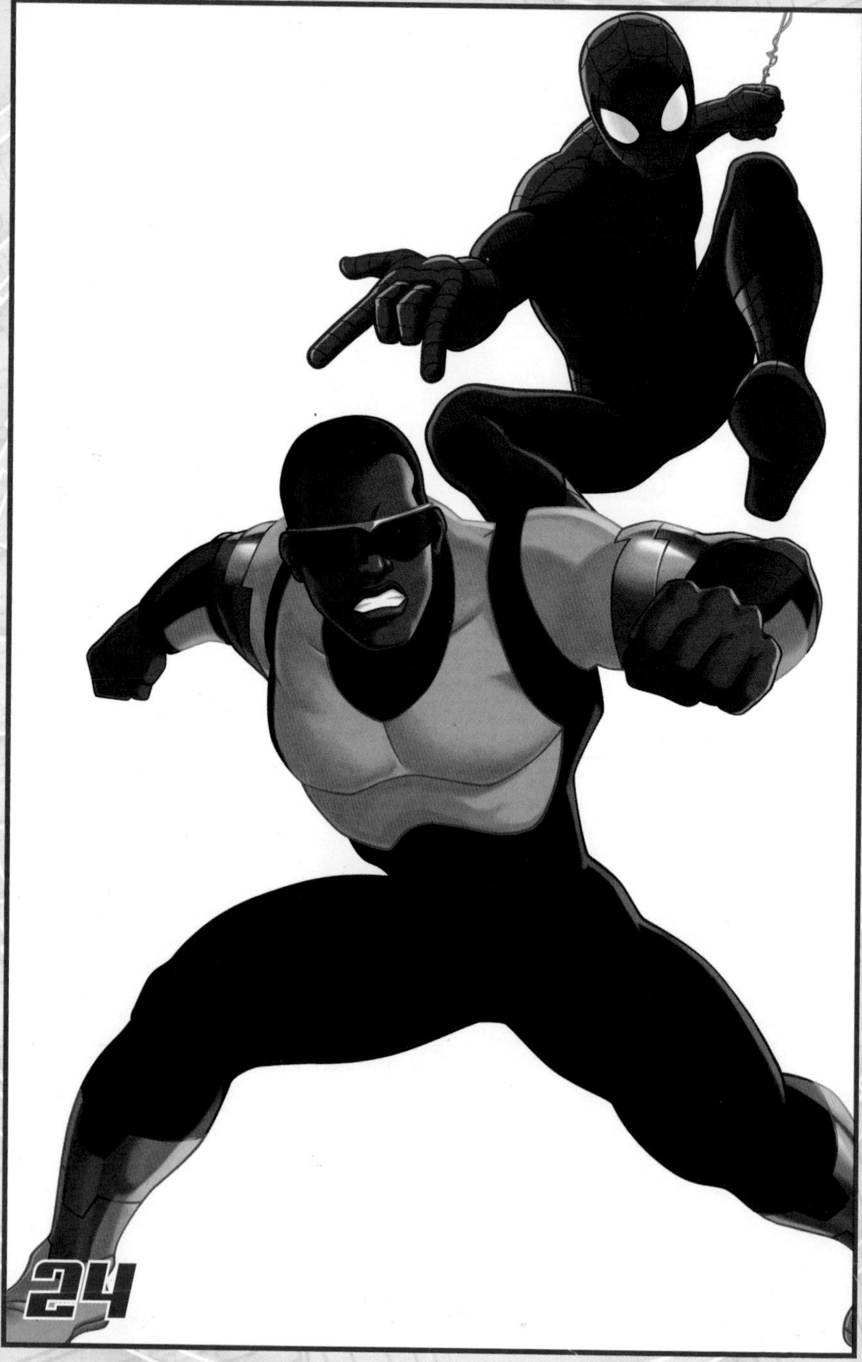

Based on "Awesome"

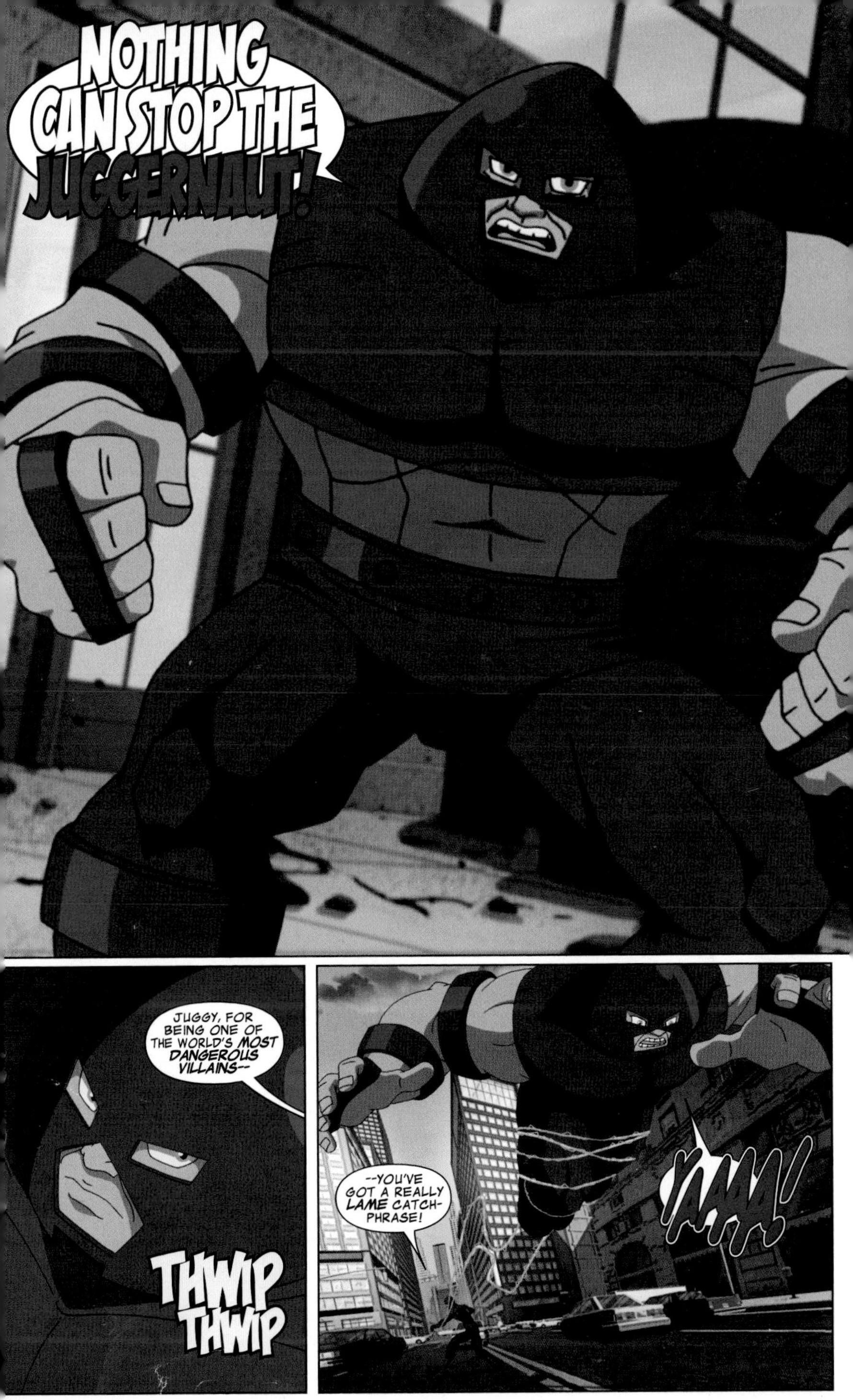
NOTHING CAN STOP THE JUGGERNAUT!
JUGGY, FOR BEING ONE OF THE WORLD'S MOST DANGEROUS VILLAINS--
THWIP THWIP
--YOU'VE GOT A REALLY LAME CATCH-PHRASE!
YAAAA!

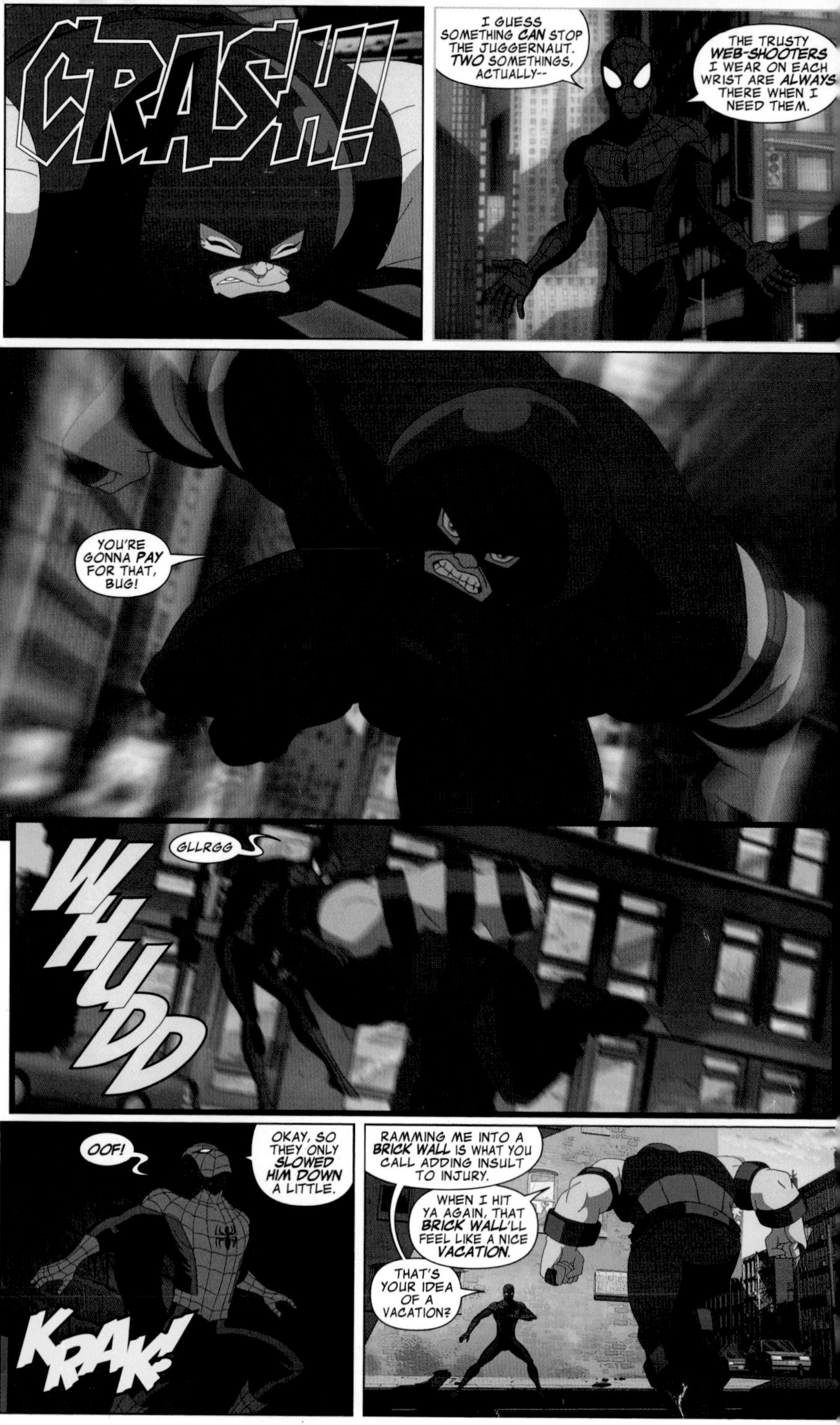
CRASH!
I GUESS SOMETHING CAN STOP THE JUGGERNAUT. TWO SOMETHINGS, ACTUALLY--
THE TRUSTY WEB-SHOOTERS I WEAR ON EACH WRIST ARE ALWAYS THERE WHEN I NEED THEM.
YOU'RE GONNA PAY FOR THAT, BUG!
GLLRGG
WHUDD
OOF!
OKAY, SO THEY ONLY SLOWED HIM DOWN A LITTLE.
KRAK!
RAMMING ME INTO A BRICK WALL IS WHAT YOU CALL ADDING INSULT TO INJURY.
WHEN I HIT YA AGAIN, THAT BRICK WALL'LL FEEL LIKE A NICE VACATION.
THAT'S YOUR IDEA OF A VACATION?

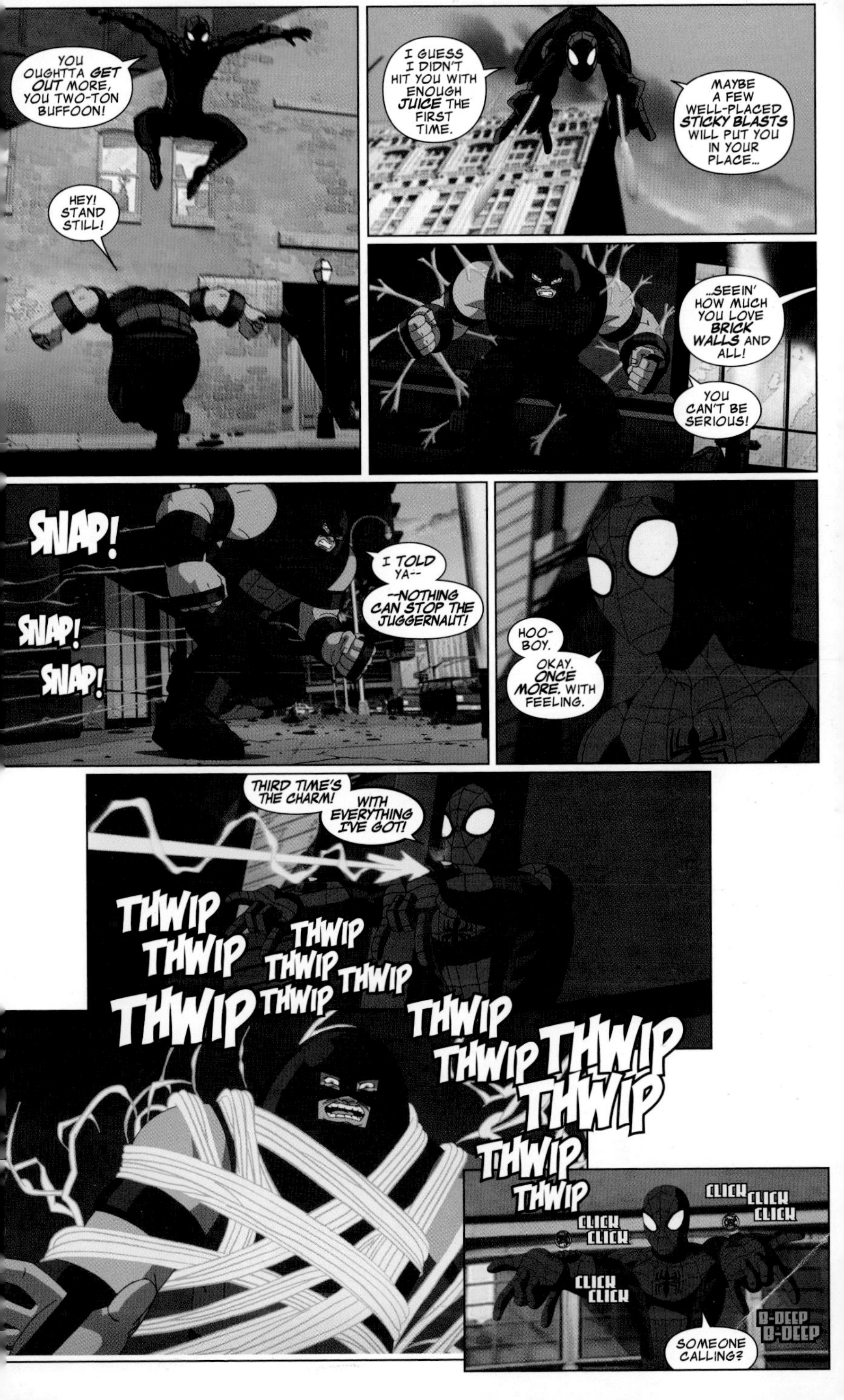
YOU OUGHTTA GET OUT MORE, YOU TWO-TON BUFFOON!
HEY! STAND STILL!
I GUESS I DIDN'T HIT YOU WITH ENOUGH JUICE THE FIRST TIME.
MAYBE A FEW WELL-PLACED STICKY BLASTS WILL PUT YOU IN YOUR PLACE...
...SEEIN' HOW MUCH YOU LOVE BRICK WALLS AND ALL!
YOU CAN'T BE SERIOUS!
SNAP!
SNAP!
SNAP!
I TOLD YA--
--NOTHING CAN STOP THE JUGGERNAUT!
HOO-BOY.
OKAY. ONCE MORE. WITH FEELING.
THIRD TIME'S THE CHARM!
WITH EVERYTHING I'VE GOT!
THWIP THWIP THWIP
THWIP THWIP THWIP THWIP
THWIP THWIP THWIP THWIP THWIP THWIP
CLICK CLICK CLICK
CLICK CLICK
CLICK CLICK
B-DEEP B-DEEP
SOMEONE CALLING?

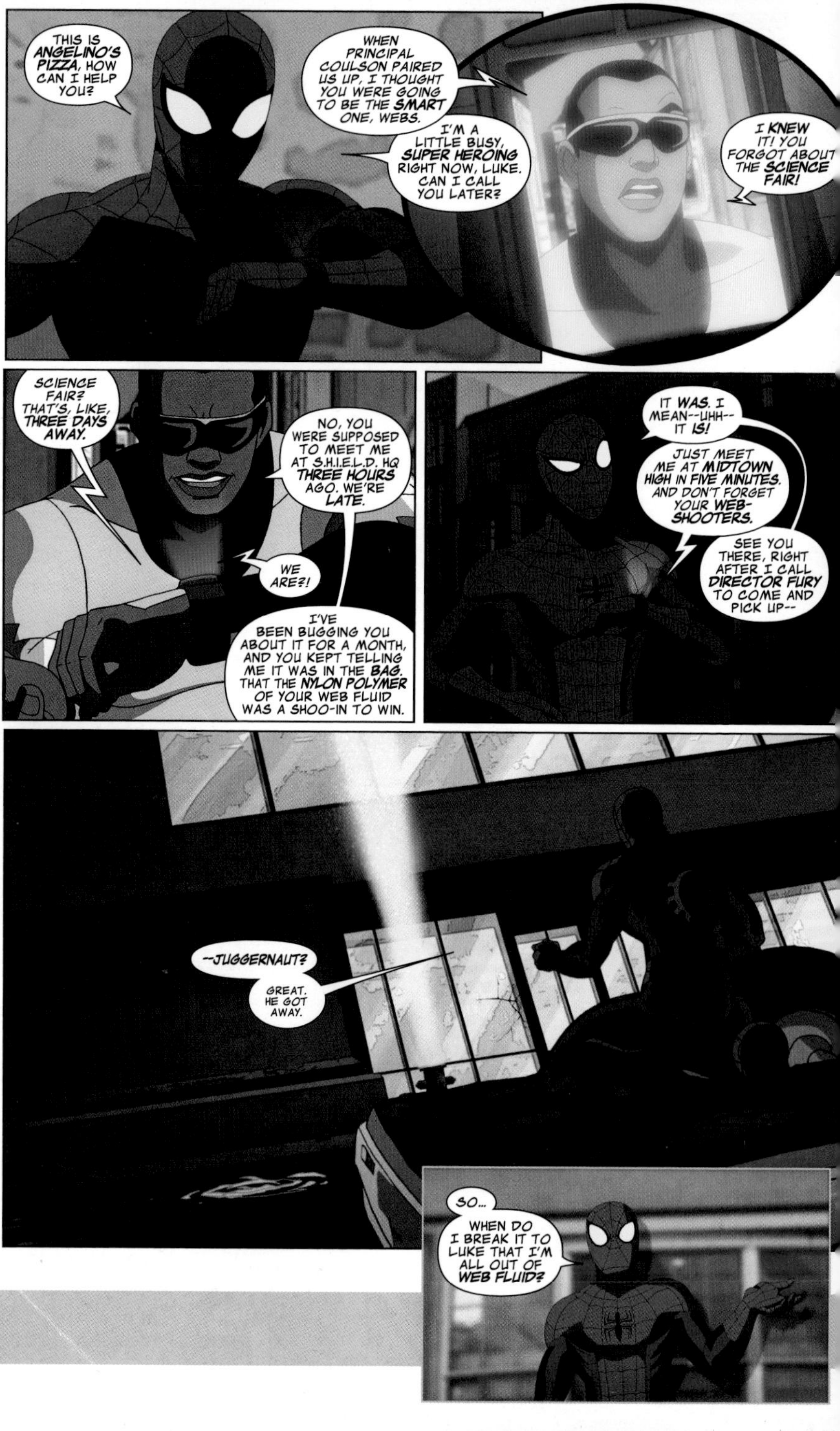
THIS IS ANGELINO'S PIZZA, HOW CAN I HELP YOU?
WHEN PRINCIPAL COULSON PAIRED US UP, I THOUGHT YOU WERE GOING TO BE THE SMART ONE, WEBS.
I'M A LITTLE BUSY, SUPER HEROING RIGHT NOW, LUKE. CAN I CALL YOU LATER?
I KNEW IT! YOU FORGOT ABOUT THE SCIENCE FAIR!
SCIENCE FAIR? THAT'S, LIKE, THREE DAYS AWAY.
NO, YOU WERE SUPPOSED TO MEET ME AT S.H.I.E.L.D. HQ THREE HOURS AGO. WE'RE LATE.
WE ARE?!
I'VE BEEN BUGGING YOU ABOUT IT FOR A MONTH, AND YOU KEPT TELLING ME IT WAS IN THE BAG. THAT THE NYLON POLYMER OF YOUR WEB FLUID WAS A SHOO-IN TO WIN.
IT WAS. I MEAN--UHH-- IT IS!
JUST MEET ME AT MIDTOWN HIGH IN FIVE MINUTES. AND DON'T FORGET YOUR WEB-SHOOTERS.
SEE YOU THERE, RIGHT AFTER I CALL DIRECTOR FURY TO COME AND PICK UP--
--JUGGERNAUT?
GREAT. HE GOT AWAY.
SO...
WHEN DO I BREAK IT TO LUKE THAT I'M ALL OUT OF WEB FLUID?

S.H.I.E.L.D. HELICARRIER.

OKAY. PLAN B.

NO TIME TO MAKE MORE WEB FLUID FROM SCRATCH, BUT THERE'S GOTTA BE *SOMETHING* IN DR. CONNORS' LAB I CAN USE.

HE DID SAY THAT HIS DOOR WAS ALWAYS OPEN TO ME.

NAH. TOO TINY.

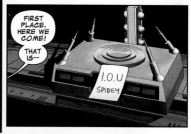

TOO BRIGHT.

WHAT IS THIS? SOME KIND OF "MOON BRICK?"

AWESOME!

FIRST PLACE, HERE WE COME!

THAT IS--

I.O.U

SPIDEY

"--IF I CAN GET THERE ON TIME!"

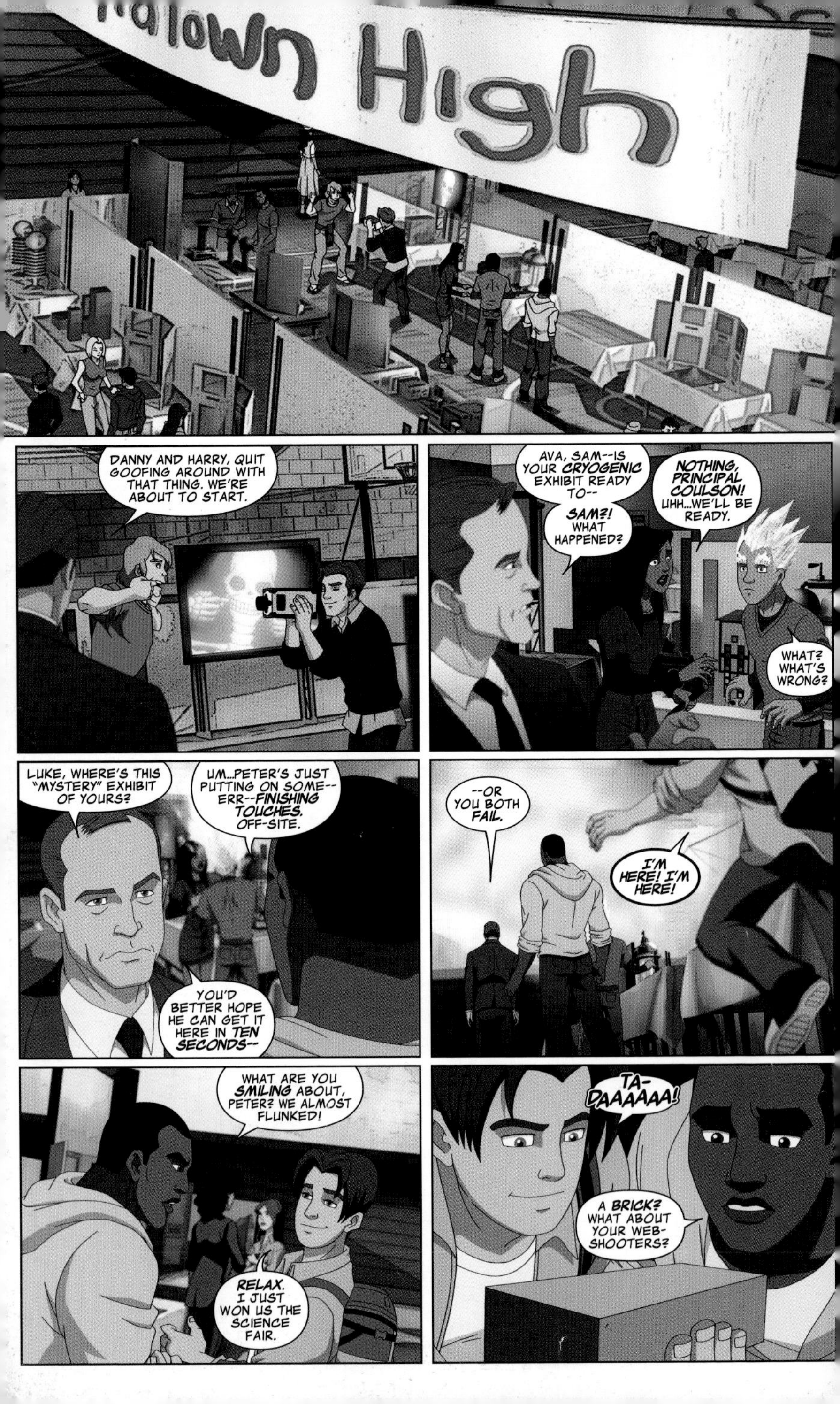
...town High
DANNY AND HARRY, QUIT GOOFING AROUND WITH THAT THING. WE'RE ABOUT TO START.
AVA, SAM--IS YOUR CRYOGENIC EXHIBIT READY TO--
SAM?! WHAT HAPPENED?
NOTHING, PRINCIPAL COULSON! UHH...WE'LL BE READY.
WHAT? WHAT'S WRONG?
LUKE, WHERE'S THIS "MYSTERY" EXHIBIT OF YOURS?
UM...PETER'S JUST PUTTING ON SOME--ERR--FINISHING TOUCHES. OFF-SITE.
YOU'D BETTER HOPE HE CAN GET IT HERE IN TEN SECONDS--
--OR YOU BOTH FAIL.
I'M HERE! I'M HERE!
WHAT ARE YOU SMILING ABOUT, PETER? WE ALMOST FLUNKED!
RELAX. I JUST WON US THE SCIENCE FAIR.
TA-DAAAAAA!
A BRICK? WHAT ABOUT YOUR WEB-SHOOTERS?

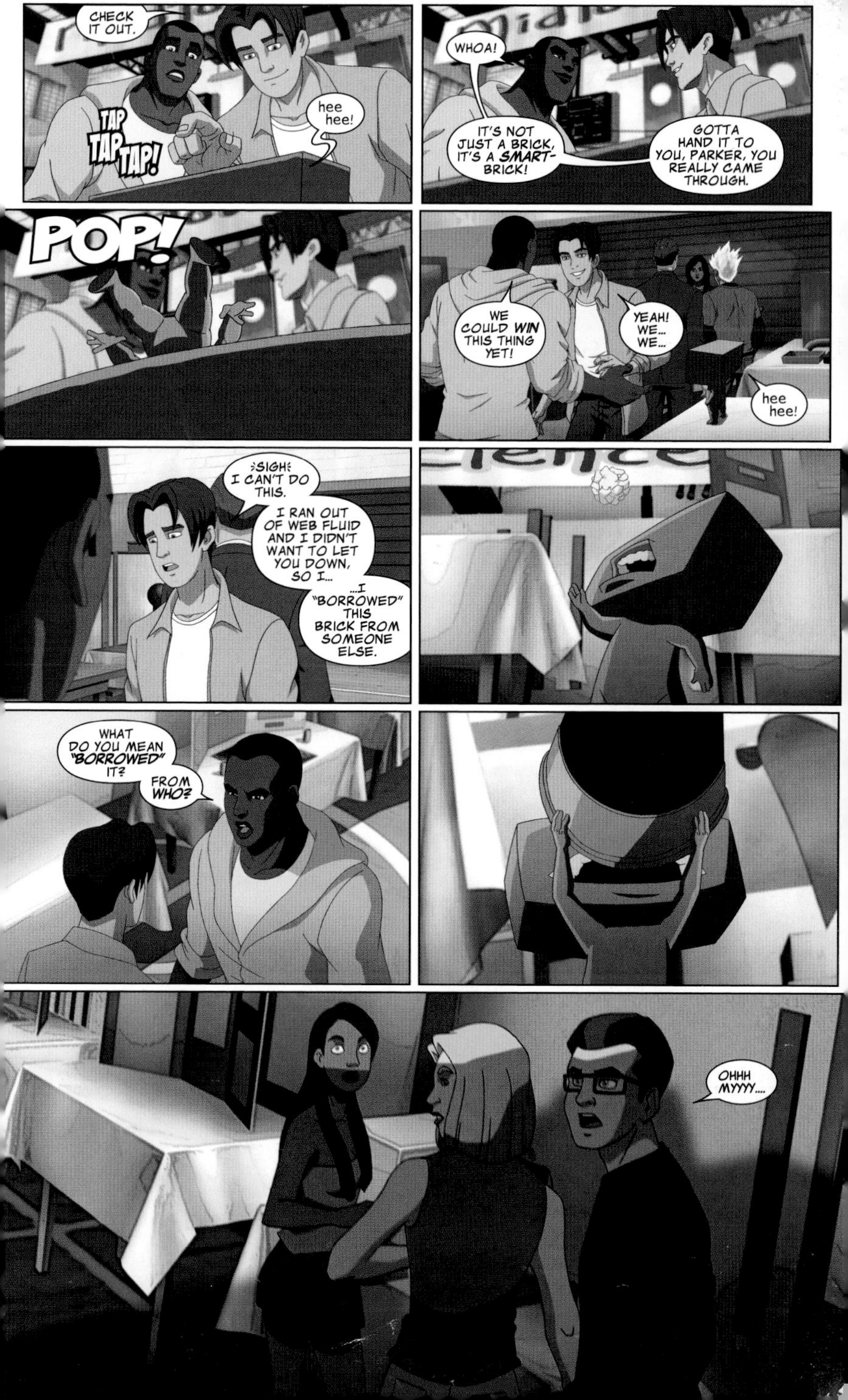
CHECK IT OUT.
TAP TAP TAP!
hee hee!
WHOA!
IT'S NOT JUST A BRICK, IT'S A SMART-BRICK!
GOTTA HAND IT TO YOU, PARKER, YOU REALLY CAME THROUGH.
POP!
WE COULD WIN THIS THING YET!
YEAH! WE... WE...
hee hee!
SIGH I CAN'T DO THIS.
I RAN OUT OF WEB FLUID AND I DIDN'T WANT TO LET YOU DOWN, SO I...
...I "BORROWED" THIS BRICK FROM SOMEONE ELSE.
WHAT DO YOU MEAN "BORROWED" IT?
FROM WHO?
OHHH MYYYY....

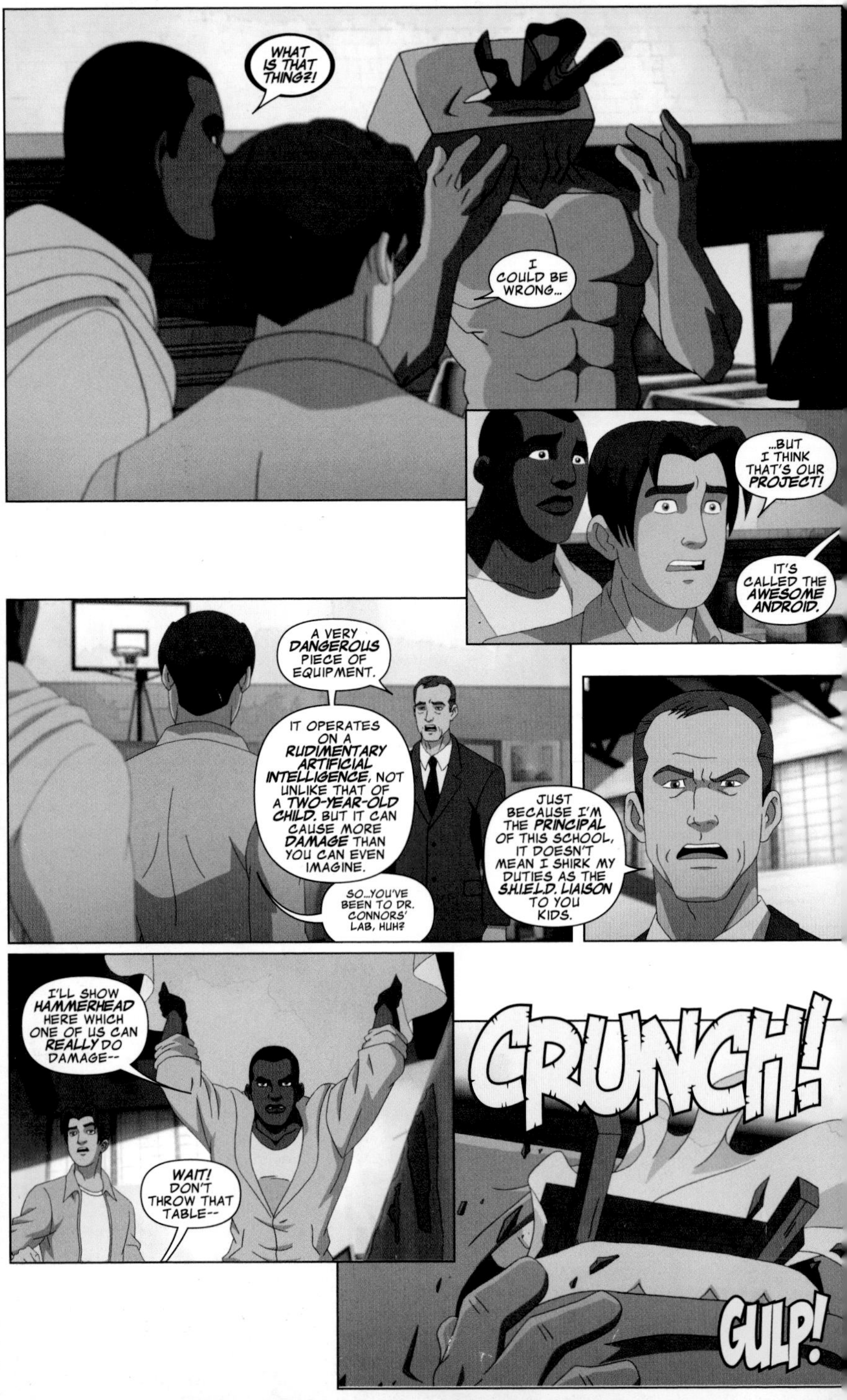
WHAT IS THAT THING?!
I COULD BE WRONG...
...BUT I THINK THAT'S OUR PROJECT!
IT'S CALLED THE AWESOME ANDROID.
A VERY DANGEROUS PIECE OF EQUIPMENT.
IT OPERATES ON A RUDIMENTARY ARTIFICIAL INTELLIGENCE, NOT UNLIKE THAT OF A TWO-YEAR-OLD CHILD. BUT IT CAN CAUSE MORE DAMAGE THAN YOU CAN EVEN IMAGINE.
SO...YOU'VE BEEN TO DR. CONNORS' LAB, HUH?
JUST BECAUSE I'M THE PRINCIPAL OF THIS SCHOOL, IT DOESN'T MEAN I SHIRK MY DUTIES AS THE S.H.I.E.L.D. LIAISON TO YOU KIDS.
I'LL SHOW HAMMERHEAD HERE WHICH ONE OF US CAN REALLY DO DAMAGE--
WAIT! DON'T THROW THAT TABLE--
CRUNCH!
GULP!

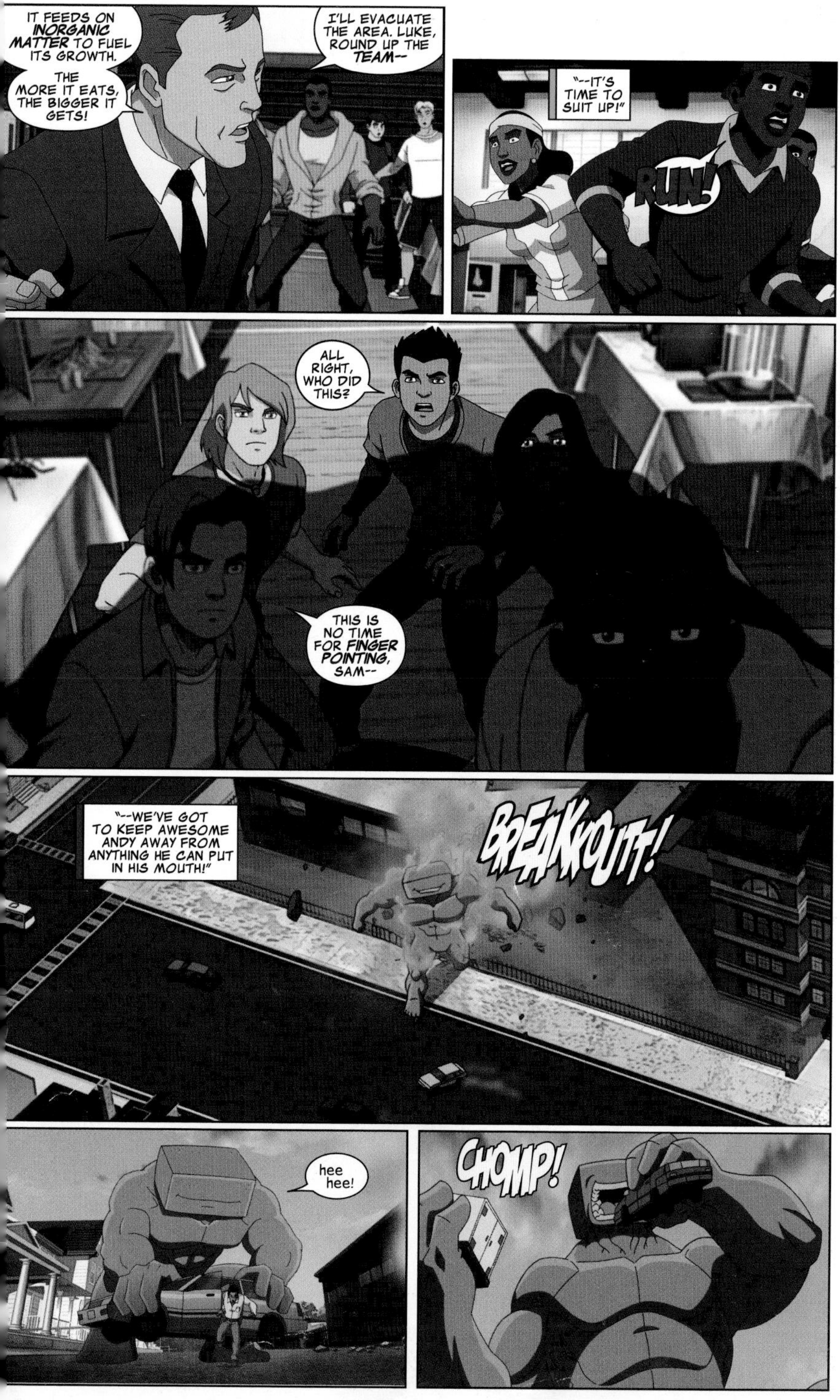
IT FEEDS ON INORGANIC MATTER TO FUEL ITS GROWTH.
THE MORE IT EATS, THE BIGGER IT GETS!
I'LL EVACUATE THE AREA. LUKE, ROUND UP THE TEAM--
"--IT'S TIME TO SUIT UP!"
RUN!
ALL RIGHT, WHO DID THIS?
THIS IS NO TIME FOR FINGER POINTING, SAM--
"--WE'VE GOT TO KEEP AWESOME ANDY AWAY FROM ANYTHING HE CAN PUT IN HIS MOUTH!"
BREAKOUT!
hee hee!
CHOMP!

WHOA! LITTLE ANDY'S ALL GROWN UP.

AND GETTING BIGGER BY THE MINUTE! HOW ARE WE GONNA STOP IT FROM EATING?

HOOOOOOHHOOOOO!

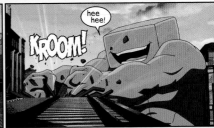

hee hee!

KROOM!

"FOR STARTERS, LET'S STOP HIM FROM *EATING* THAT TRAIN!"

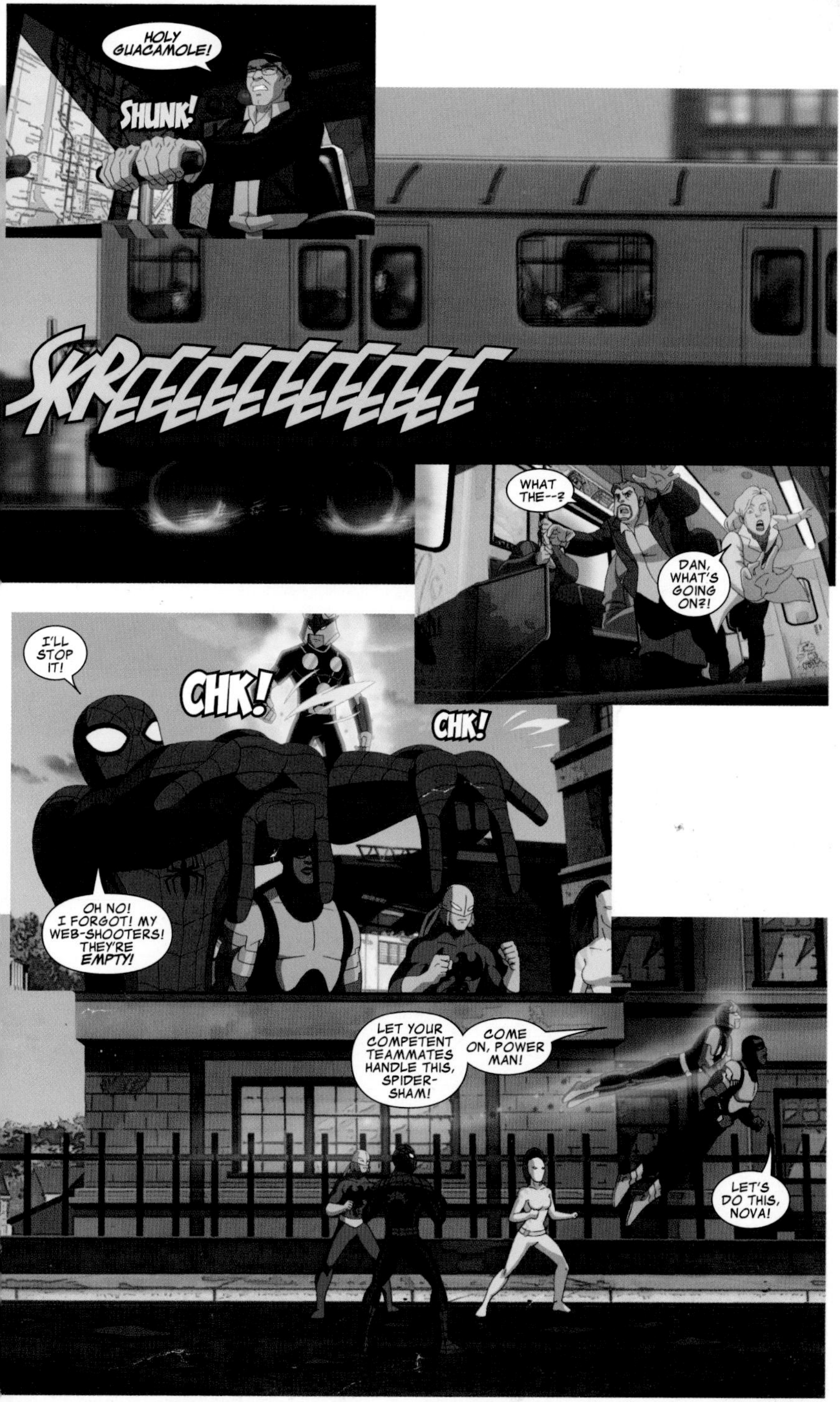
HOLY GUACAMOLE!
SHUNK!
SKREEEEEEEEEEEEE
WHAT THE--?
DAN, WHAT'S GOING ON?!
I'LL STOP IT!
CHK!
CHK!
OH NO! I FORGOT! MY WEB-SHOOTERS! THEY'RE EMPTY!
LET YOUR COMPETENT TEAMMATES HANDLE THIS, SPIDER-SHAM!
COME ON, POWER MAN!
LET'S DO THIS, NOVA!

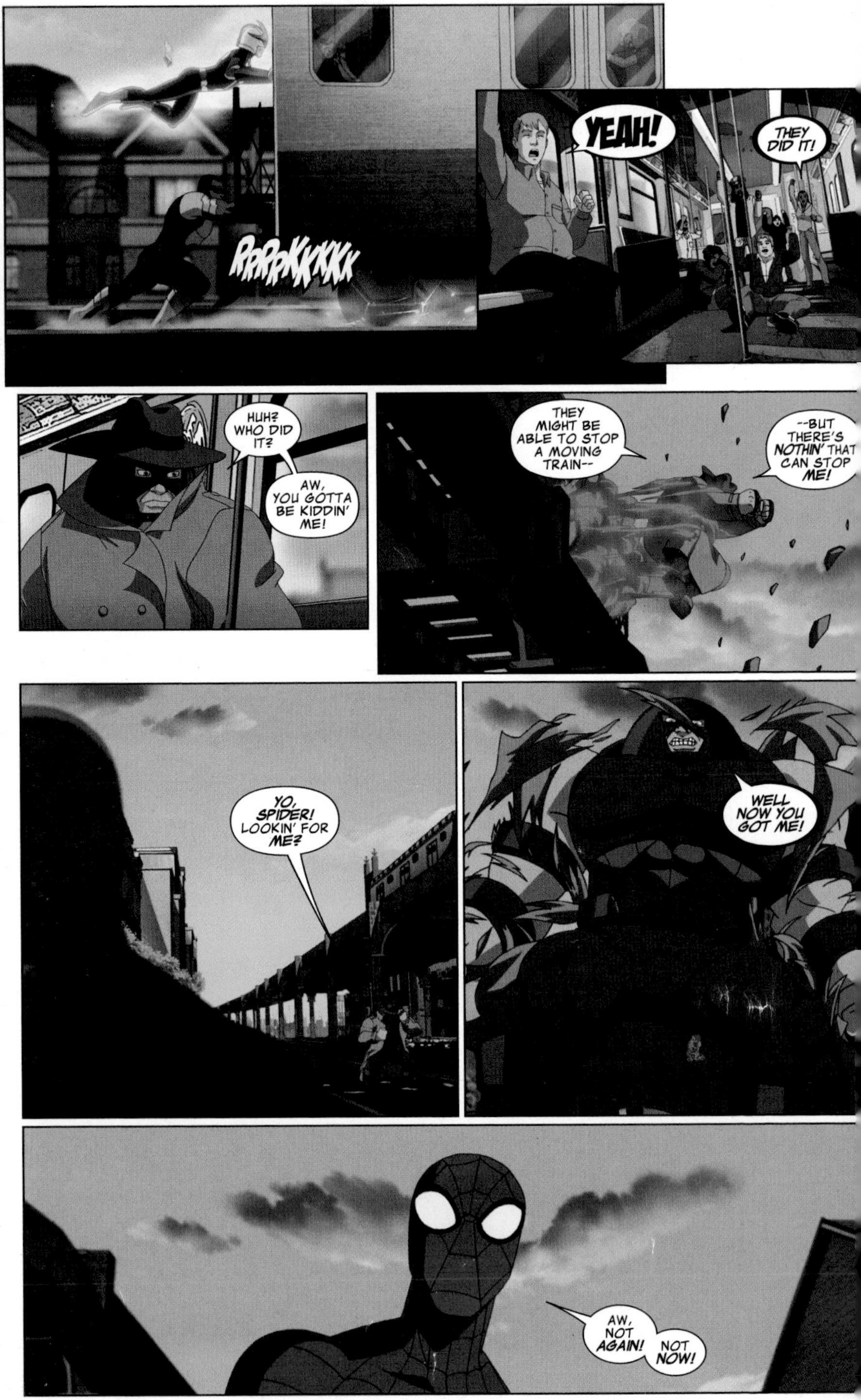
RRRRKKKKK
YEAH!
THEY DID IT!
HUH? WHO DID IT?
AW, YOU GOTTA BE KIDDIN' ME!
THEY MIGHT BE ABLE TO STOP A MOVING TRAIN--
--BUT THERE'S NOTHIN' THAT CAN STOP ME!
YO, SPIDER! LOOKIN' FOR ME?
WELL NOW YOU GOT ME!
AW, NOT AGAIN!
NOT NOW!

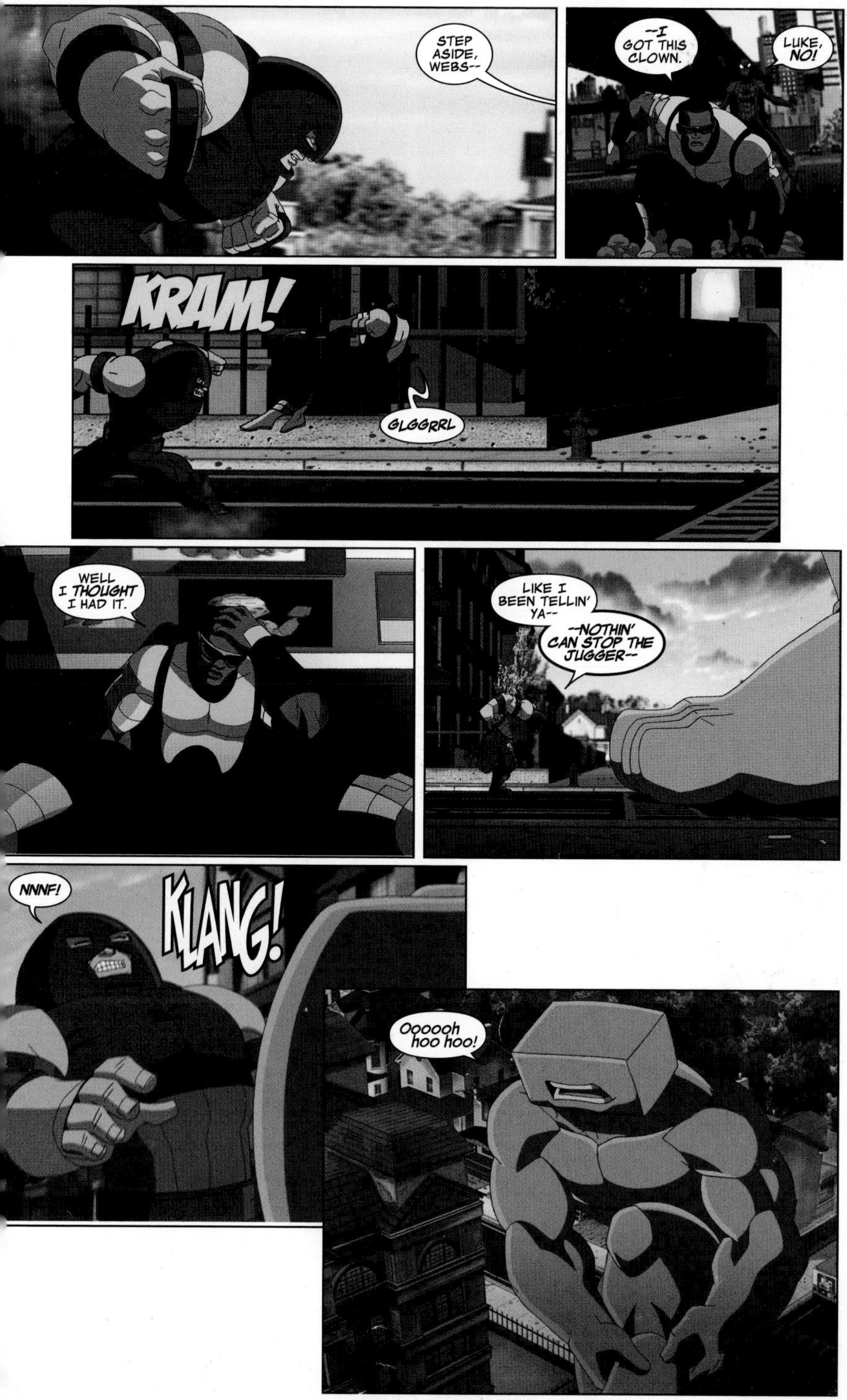
STEP ASIDE, WEBS--
--I GOT THIS CLOWN.
LUKE, NO!
KRAM!
GLGGRRL
WELL I THOUGHT I HAD IT.
LIKE I BEEN TELLIN' YA--
--NOTHIN' CAN STOP THE JUGGER--
NNNF!
KLANG!
Oooooh hoo hoo!

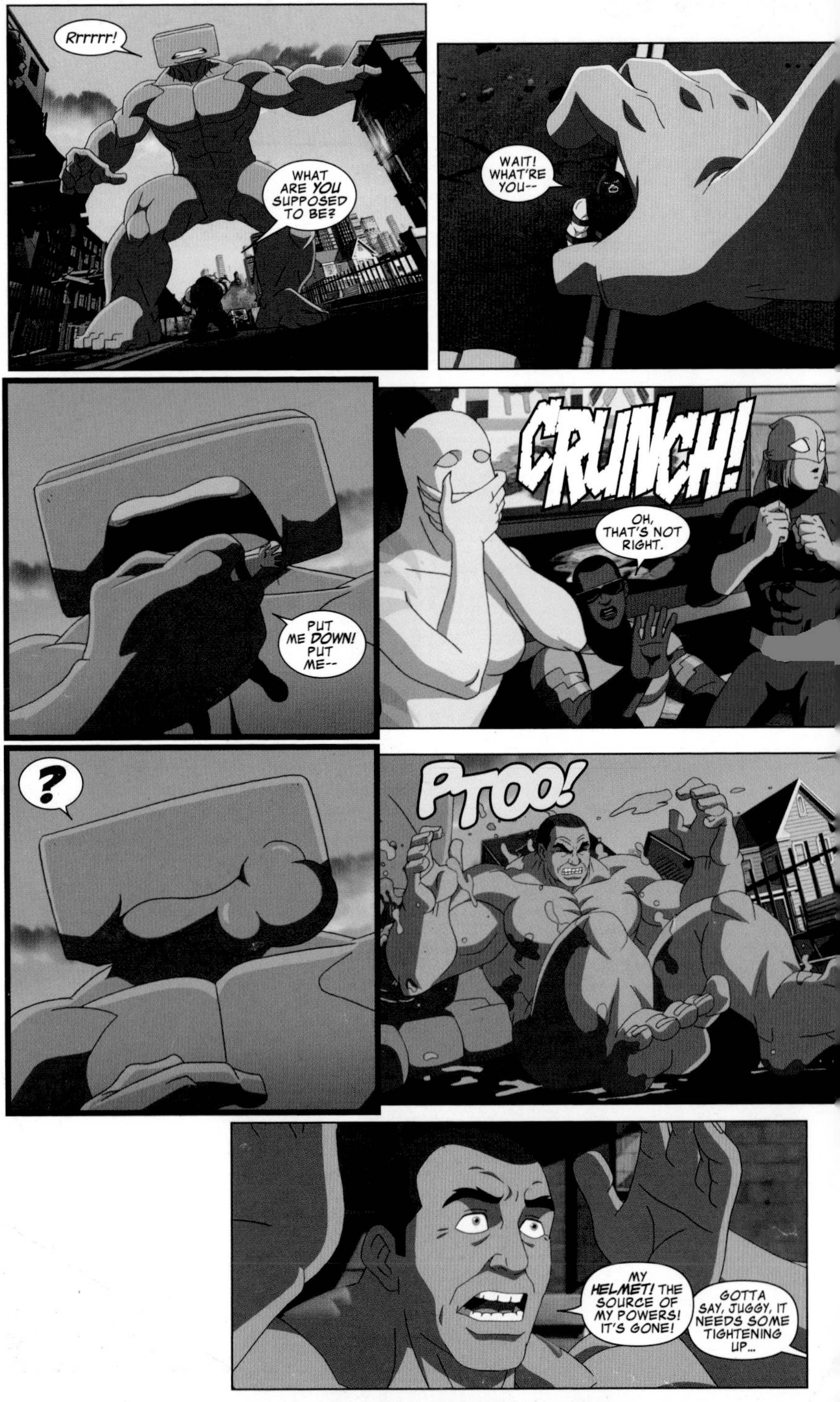
Rrrrrr!
WHAT ARE YOU SUPPOSED TO BE?
WAIT! WHAT'RE YOU--
PUT ME DOWN! PUT ME--
CRUNCH!
OH, THAT'S NOT RIGHT.
?
PTOO!
MY HELMET! THE SOURCE OF MY POWERS! IT'S GONE!
GOTTA SAY, JUGGY, IT NEEDS SOME TIGHTENING UP...

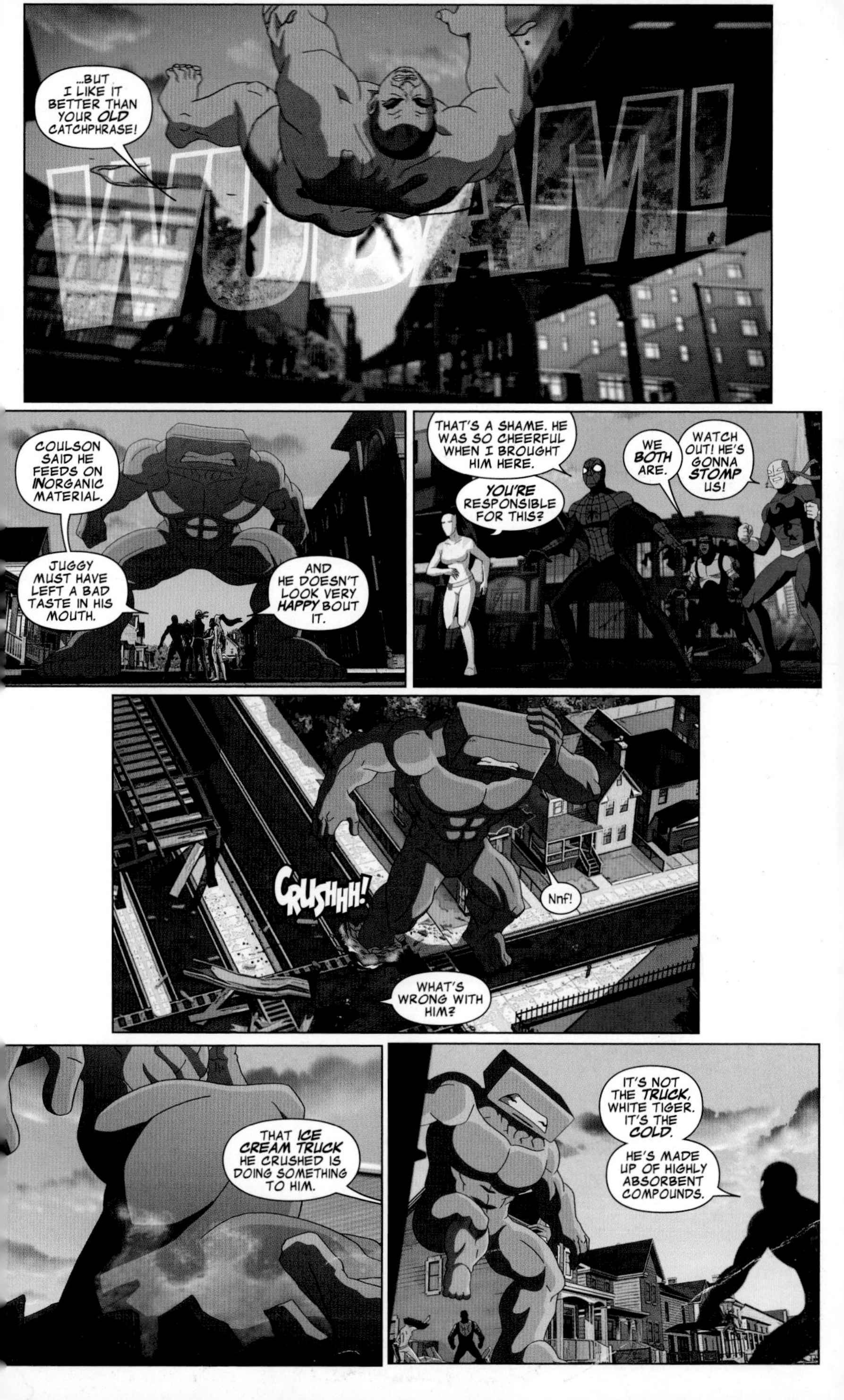

...BUT I LIKE IT BETTER THAN YOUR OLD CATCHPHRASE!
WUDAAM!
COULSON SAID HE FEEDS ON INORGANIC MATERIAL.
JUGGY MUST HAVE LEFT A BAD TASTE IN HIS MOUTH.
AND HE DOESN'T LOOK VERY HAPPY BOUT IT.
THAT'S A SHAME. HE WAS SO CHEERFUL WHEN I BROUGHT HIM HERE.
YOU'RE RESPONSIBLE FOR THIS?
WE BOTH ARE.
WATCH OUT! HE'S GONNA STOMP US!
CRUSHHH!
Nnf!
WHAT'S WRONG WITH HIM?
THAT ICE CREAM TRUCK HE CRUSHED IS DOING SOMETHING TO HIM.
IT'S NOT THE TRUCK, WHITE TIGER. IT'S THE COLD.
HE'S MADE UP OF HIGHLY ABSORBENT COMPOUNDS.

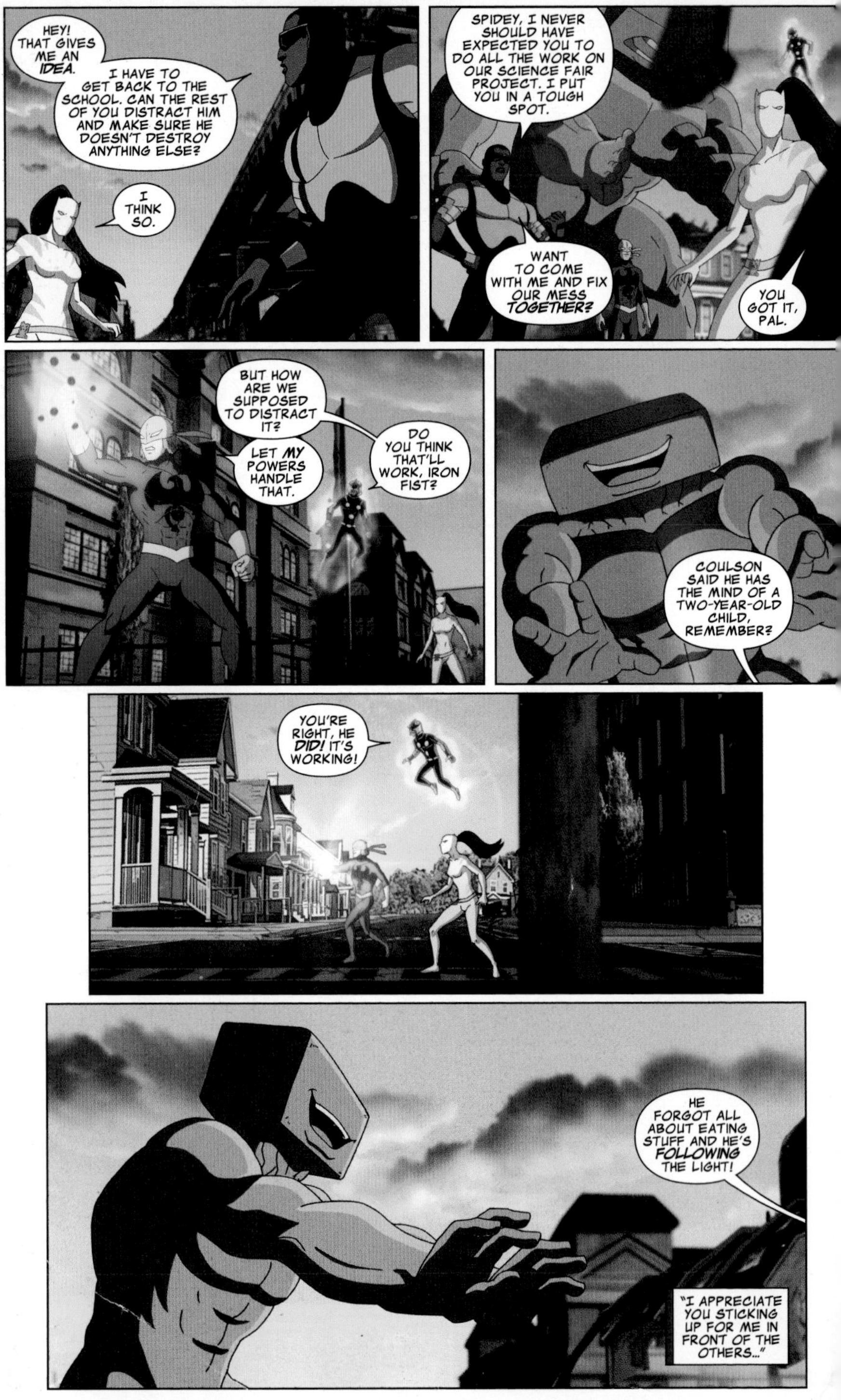
HEY! THAT GIVES ME AN IDEA.
I HAVE TO GET BACK TO THE SCHOOL. CAN THE REST OF YOU DISTRACT HIM AND MAKE SURE HE DOESN'T DESTROY ANYTHING ELSE?
I THINK SO.
SPIDEY, I NEVER SHOULD HAVE EXPECTED YOU TO DO ALL THE WORK ON OUR SCIENCE FAIR PROJECT. I PUT YOU IN A TOUGH SPOT.
WANT TO COME WITH ME AND FIX OUR MESS TOGETHER?
YOU GOT IT, PAL.
BUT HOW ARE WE SUPPOSED TO DISTRACT IT?
LET MY POWERS HANDLE THAT.
DO YOU THINK THAT'LL WORK, IRON FIST?
COULSON SAID HE HAS THE MIND OF A TWO-YEAR-OLD CHILD, REMEMBER?
YOU'RE RIGHT, HE DID! IT'S WORKING!
HE FORGOT ALL ABOUT EATING STUFF AND HE'S FOLLOWING THE LIGHT!
"I APPRECIATE YOU STICKING UP FOR ME IN FRONT OF THE OTHERS..."

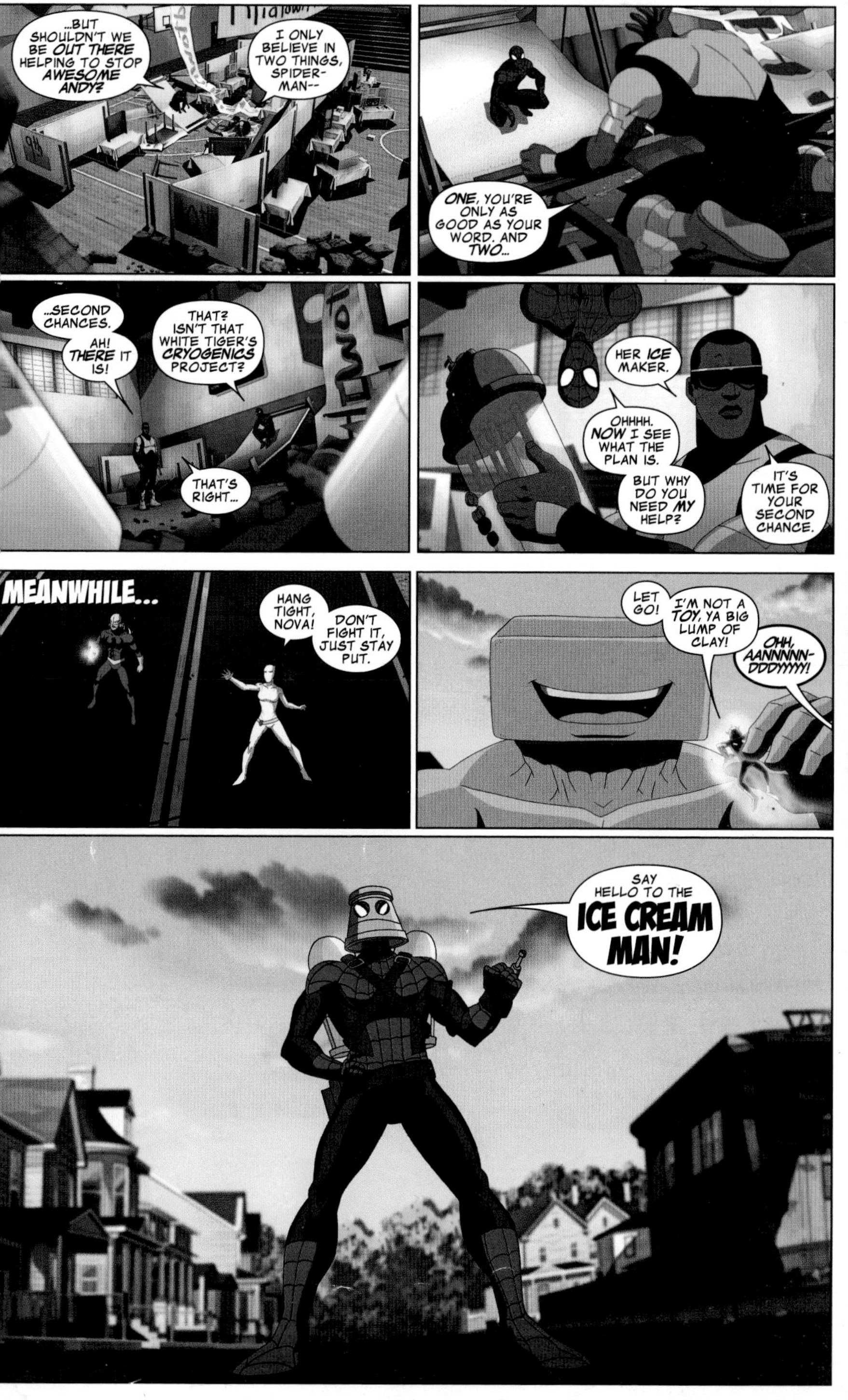
...BUT SHOULDN'T WE BE OUT THERE HELPING TO STOP AWESOME ANDY?
I ONLY BELIEVE IN TWO THINGS, SPIDER-MAN--
ONE, YOU'RE ONLY AS GOOD AS YOUR WORD. AND TWO...
...SECOND CHANCES.
AH! THERE IT IS!
THAT? ISN'T THAT WHITE TIGER'S CRYOGENICS PROJECT?
THAT'S RIGHT...
HER ICE MAKER.
OHHHH. NOW I SEE WHAT THE PLAN IS.
BUT WHY DO YOU NEED MY HELP?
IT'S TIME FOR YOUR SECOND CHANCE.
MEANWHILE...
HANG TIGHT, NOVA!
DON'T FIGHT IT, JUST STAY PUT.
LET GO!
I'M NOT A TOY, YA BIG LUMP OF CLAY!
OHH, AANNNNN-DDDYYYYY!
SAY HELLO TO THE ICE CREAM MAN!

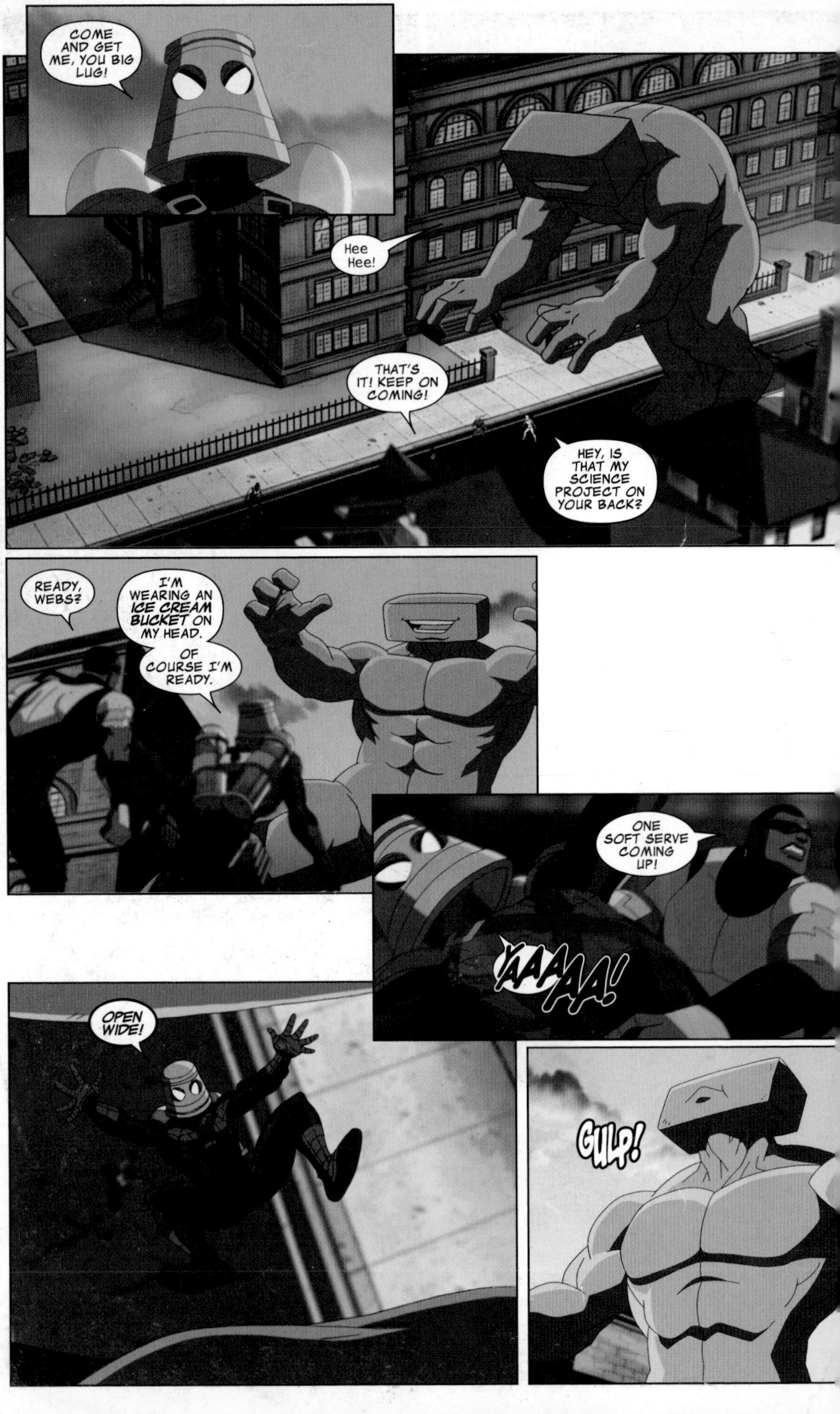
COME AND GET ME, YOU BIG LUG!
Hee Hee!
THAT'S IT! KEEP ON COMING!
HEY, IS THAT MY SCIENCE PROJECT ON YOUR BACK?
READY, WEBS?
I'M WEARING AN ICE CREAM BUCKET ON MY HEAD.
OF COURSE I'M READY.
ONE SOFT SERVE COMING UP!
YAAAAA!
OPEN WIDE!
GULP!

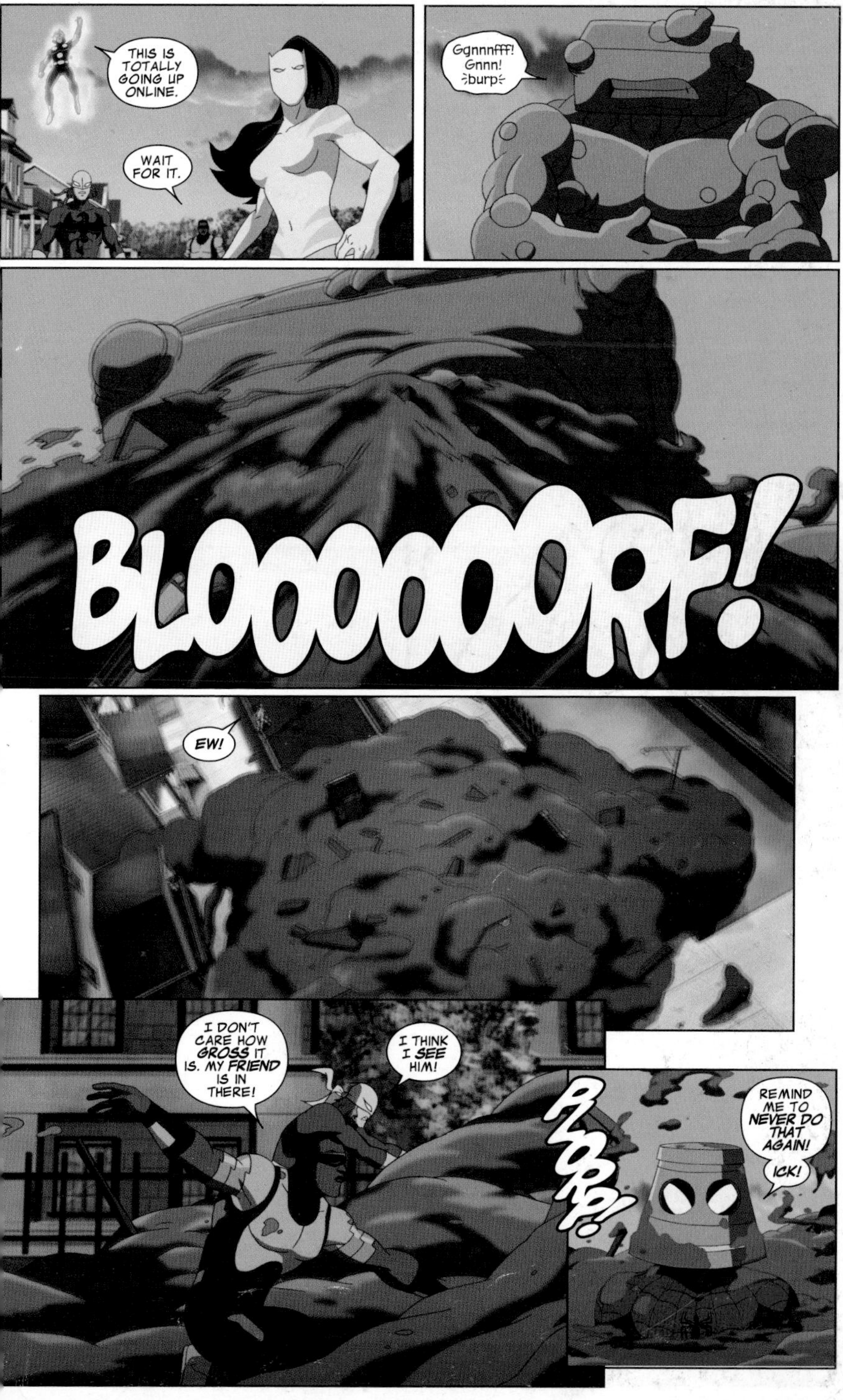

THIS IS TOTALLY GOING UP ONLINE.
WAIT FOR IT.
Ggnnnfff! Gnnn! burp
BLOOOOOORF!
EW!
I DON'T CARE HOW GROSS IT IS. MY FRIEND IS IN THERE!
I THINK I SEE HIM!
PLOOP!
REMIND ME TO NEVER DO THAT AGAIN!
ICK!

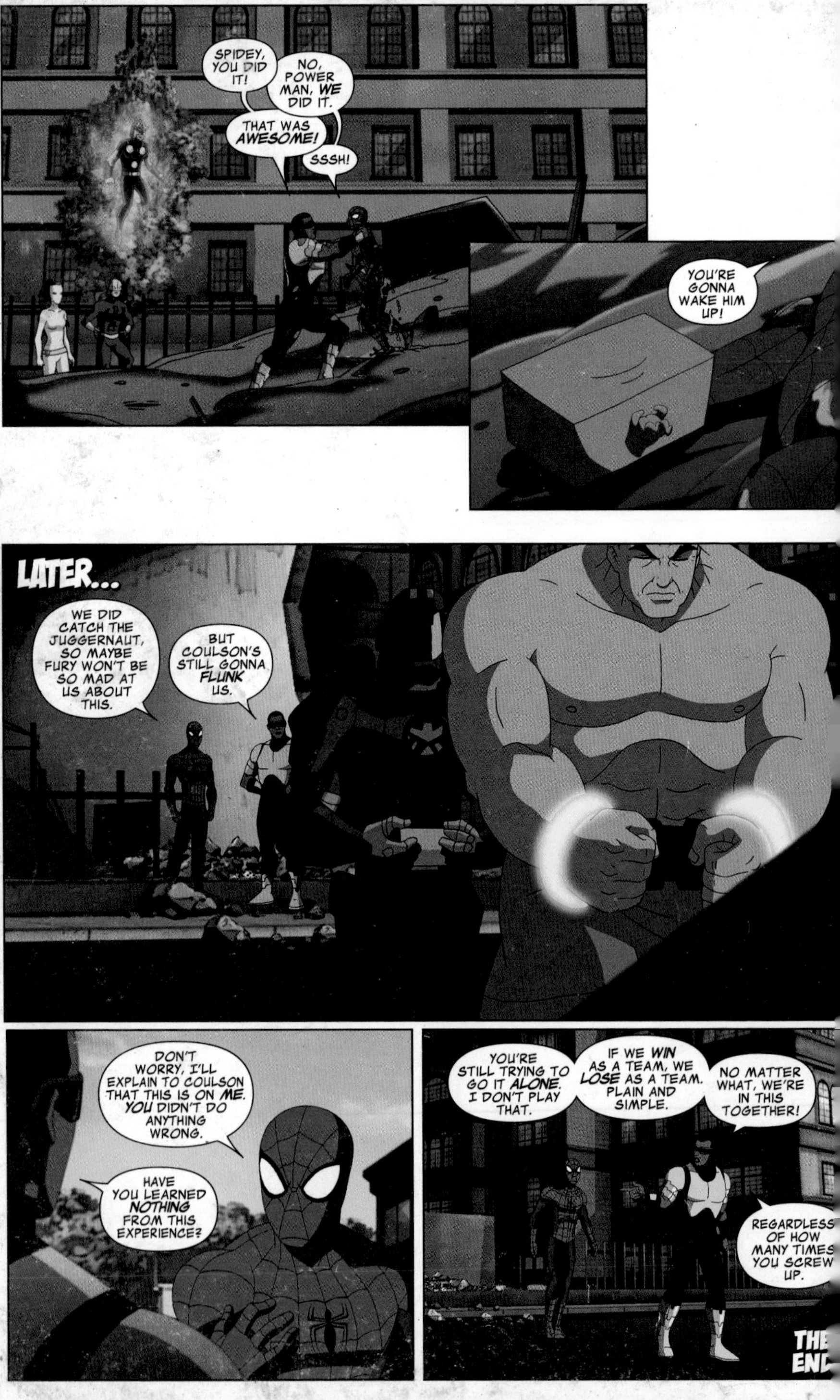

SPIDEY, YOU DID IT!
NO, POWER MAN, WE DID IT.
THAT WAS AWESOME!
SSSH!
YOU'RE GONNA WAKE HIM UP!
LATER...
WE DID CATCH THE JUGGERNAUT, SO MAYBE FURY WON'T BE SO MAD AT US ABOUT THIS.
BUT COULSON'S STILL GONNA FLUNK US.
DON'T WORRY, I'LL EXPLAIN TO COULSON THAT THIS IS ON ME. YOU DIDN'T DO ANYTHING WRONG.
HAVE YOU LEARNED NOTHING FROM THIS EXPERIENCE?
YOU'RE STILL TRYING TO GO IT ALONE. I DON'T PLAY THAT.
IF WE WIN AS A TEAM, WE LOSE AS A TEAM. PLAIN AND SIMPLE.
NO MATTER WHAT, WE'RE IN THIS TOGETHER!
REGARDLESS OF HOW MANY TIMES YOU SCREW UP.
THE END